AF767204

Man Enough

Man Enough

How to Protect Boys from Online Misogyny

MATTEO BERGAMINI MBE
AND AMELIA FAIRNEY

SOUVENIR
PRESS

First published in Great Britain in 2026 by
Souvenir Press,
an imprint of Profile Books Ltd
29 Cloth Fair
London
EC1A 7JQ
www.souvenirpress.co.uk

Copyright © Matteo Bergamini and Amelia Fairney, 2026

Typeset by seagulls.net

1 3 5 7 9 10 8 6 4 2

Printed and bound in Great Britain by
CPI Group (UK) Ltd, Croydon, CR0 4YY

The moral right of the author has been asserted.

All rights reserved. Without limiting the rights under copyright reserved above, no part of this publication may be reproduced, stored or introduced into a retrieval system, or transmitted, in any form or by any means (electronic, mechanical, photocopying, recording or otherwise), without the prior written permission of both the copyright owner and the publisher of this book.

Profile Books takes seriously the responsibility of defending our authors' copyright. No part of this book may be used or reproduced in any manner for the purpose of training artificial intelligence technologies or systems (including but not limited to machine learning models and large language models (LLMs)). In accordance with Article 4(3) of the DSM Directive 2019/790, Profile Books expressly reserves this work from the text and data mining exception.

A CIP catalogue record for this book is available from the British Library.

Our product safety representative in the EU is BGC Sustainability & Compliance, 7 avenue du Général Leclerc, Paris, 75014, France
https://baldwinglobalconsulting.com

ISBN 978 1 80522 921 6
eISBN 978 1 80522 922 3

MIX
Paper | Supporting responsible forestry
FSC® C013604

For P&P: great men. And in memory of my fellow author and bookseller, Diccon Bewes (1967–2025).

— Amelia —

For my love Sabina. And for my daughter and son, may this book contribute to you inheriting a world, and an internet, free from toxic voices.

— Matteo —

Contents

Introduction

'This path of self-improvement that I've got you on, every six months you unlock a new tier of woman.'

'Most women do not even tick half the boxes of the ideal woman you want to spend time with in your life.'

'Some people would say I disrespect women. I would say I expose women.'

'How do you become a top-tier man?'

'Women get mad at us because we reveal the game and the realities about female nature.'

'Women will only like you for what you can provide for them.'

'Powerful men all have this masculine trait.'

'How to destroy your inner nice guy.'

'Women love arrogant men. Women love dominant guys.'

These are examples of messages we found, after just a few minutes' worth of scrolling, having typed 'self-improvement for boys' into TikTok's search bar: just some random examples of the confident and commanding messages about masculinity that teenagers receive online every day. At a time when boys' bodies are changing and their hormones are surging, when they may be developing the first stirrings of sexual and romantic desire, but perhaps feeling insecure about their own attractiveness, there are many men on social media who are keen to teach them what a successful male looks like.

So what? you may ask. What's wrong with boys seeking out advice on how to get fit, meet girls and succeed in life? The answer lies in the business model of social media. In 2026, a BBC investigation interviewed whistle-blowers at TikTok and Meta who confirmed that over the past several years, their companies, engaged in what the BBC called an 'algorithm arms race', had made decisions to optimise users' feeds for extreme and polarising content that kept them engaged longer.[1] Some of that content, viewed daily by thousands of boys in the UK, has been promoting highly divisive and harmful messages about women and girls.* As we've just shown above, boys don't need to look far to come across posts pushing negative stereotypes. And once a boy has clicked on one video, he will likely be rapidly served up far worse. In fact, a recent survey found 69 per cent of eleven- to

* A note on language: we will use the binary terms: 'girls', 'boys', 'women' and 'men' throughout this book since these are most widely used across the data sources we've researched. We want to make clear that gender-nonconforming, trans and non-binary people are also frequently victims and targets of online misogyny, which is homophobic and transphobic to its core.

fourteen-year-old boys have been exposed to content promoting misogyny and other extremist views while scrolling.[2]

Over the last hundred years or so, we've seen great progress in women's rights. After centuries of being denied a right to a vote, education or career, feminist pioneers paved the way for the current state of affairs, where, in many countries, we take women's full participation in society for granted. But, since the turn of the millennium, we've seen an increasing backlash against the advances of feminism. Women's progress in education, the professions, and in freely expressing their sexuality and reproductive rights has been framed by some politicians, commentators and social media personalities as coming at the expense of the well-being of boys and men, who, it is argued, find themselves falling behind educationally and economically, and disproportionately and unfairly blamed for society's ills.*

While sometimes rooted in men's legitimate anxieties about their lives, this narrative of women's rights as a zero-sum game in which men lose out has, in recent years, been given a huge boost by the ease of online communication. The rise of social media has brought an almost infinite variety of voices into the digitally connected lives of young people – some of them, in an under-moderated internet, keen to allocate blame to women in the most hateful terms.

In 2024, Hope Not Hate found that 41 per cent of men aged sixteen to twenty-four in the UK had a positive view of the

* US sociologist Michael Kimmel explores this backlash in his 2017 book, *Angry White Men*. It springs, he suggests, from what he calls a sense of 'aggrieved entitlement' from men who feel their natural privileges have been usurped by the social changes of deindustrialisation and feminism.

internet's misogynist-in-chief, Andrew Tate, and 95 per cent knew who he was.[3] In a world where teenagers often place a huge amount of trust in the views of social media influencers, this may partly explain why the youngest generation of men appear to be hardening against women's equality.* Data from 2026 showed that, worldwide, 59 per cent of Gen Z men feel that they are asked to do too much to support gender equality, with 57 per cent feeling it has gone so far that it discriminates against men; 31 per cent expressed the view that 'a wife should always obey her husband' compared to just 13 per cent of baby boomers. Apparently, young men look less favourably on feminism than older generations.[4]

A slew of recent data appears to show that rising levels of online misogyny are having a catastrophic real-world impact on girls and women. In 2021, Ofsted's rapid review into sexual harassment and abuse at schools found evidence that peer-to-peer harassment was commonplace and that sexism frequently remained unchallenged by children's school peers or staff.[5] A 2024 National Policing statement reported that recorded crimes of violence against women and girls (VAWG) had increased by 37 per cent over the previous five years – a situation it described as an 'epidemic'.[6] Women and girls also feel increasingly unsafe. In 2025, 86 per cent of women and girls aged eleven to twenty-one surveyed by Girlguiding said they had avoided going out after dark alone and 68 per cent had changed their behaviour to avoid sexual harassment.[7]

* A report by Channel 4 in 2025 found 42 per cent of thirteen- to twenty-seven-year-olds trusted internet personalities and influencers compared to 8 per cent of twenty-eight- to sixty-five-year-olds (*Gen Z: Trends, Truth and Trust*, Channel 4, January 2025).

On International Men's Day in 2025, the UK government announced it would be holding a national summit on men and boys, which was specifically framed as part of its strategy to combat VAWG, with Deputy Prime Minister David Lammy stating that men and boys 'have to be part of this conversation'.[8]

As parents, and professionals working in media literacy education, we have looked on despairingly, as what could be positive, creative and life-enhancing spaces for our kids have been ruthlessly transformed into radicalisation engines driving hostility to women. Over the last couple of years, much-discussed TV programmes such as Louis Theroux's *Inside the Manosphere* and Jack Thorne and Stephen Graham's harrowing Netflix series *Adolescence* have shone a light on something we've understood for some time through our work at Shout Out UK: ever younger boys are being targeted and indoctrinated by the hateful ideology of misogyny. And right now, parents have little idea how to prevent it.

Something clearly needs to change. Generations Z and Alpha have been guinea pigs in a global behavioural experiment: given extensive access at an early age to the fast-paced information superhighway, with its many dangerous diversions and misleading signposts, most are spending several hours online by the time they hit secondary school. But our education and parenting norms have not kept pace. We aren't yet doing enough to equip kids with the critical resilience to distinguish between harmless entertainment and content that aims to manipulate and sometimes even radicalise them.

Parents' groups and policy-makers have responded with alarm to the online harms children are experiencing – of which the normalisation of online misogyny is just one. The Smartphone

Free Childhood movement has grown over the space of two years from one parents' WhatsApp group to a campaign that has signed up parents at more than 12,000 schools to its phone-free pledge. Other options currently being put forward around the world to mitigate internet harms include social media bans for under-sixteens – already law in Australia and at the time of writing due to be implemented in the UK – compulsory screen time restrictions, and increased regulation to make tech features less addictive and moderate harmful algorithms.

We think that the latter would certainly be a positive step in protecting kids from the worst excesses of criminal and harmful behaviour on the internet. But even the most draconian social media bans will not prevent children from venturing into harmful online spaces – in fact, we'd argue that a blanket ban may drive them to darker, less moderated sites. We believe that tighter regulation must go alongside equipping boys and young men, and their parents and carers, with the basic critical skills to resist falling into the toxic trap of online misogyny. Its frightening real-world impact on women's lives is becoming too serious to do otherwise. The time to act is now.

Our core mission at Shout Out UK is to inoculate young people from online misinformation by teaching them how to use media literacy tools and techniques. Media literacy is the framework we use to analyse messages that we find online and offline. We build this framework by strengthening our critical thinking skills to question online sources of information. Our SOUK teaching resources also improve emotional resilience so young people are better able to resist the emotive messaging that is used to spread misinformation and disinformation.

Our team visits schools and other educational settings every day to deliver this training to children and young people. We work to ensure that all students, regardless of their socio-economic background, ethnicity or gender, leave our programmes with increased critical thinking skills, analytical abilities, emotional resilience and confidence, empowering them to engage thoughtfully and responsibly in all online media environments.

Our work in schools, which includes training teachers, has never been more in demand. Educators in every part of the UK recognise the value of media literacy as a vital twenty-first-century skill for our young citizens. Over the past two years, in response to their wider concern at rising levels of classroom misogyny (including, sadly, some of our own team's personal experiences), we have developed new resources, specifically tackling these attitudes among boys and young men. We know, as we both have kids ourselves, that parents are as anxious as teachers about this state of affairs. We hope that this book will bridge the current knowledge gap by providing a comprehensive and practical guide for anxious adults to the landscape of the online manosphere and what can be done to combat its influence.

We are a mum and a dad from two different generations: Matteo, a millennial who grew up alongside the internet, and Amelia, the mother of a Gen Z young man, and one of the first generation to raise a 'social media native' child. Our objective in writing this book is to draw on these dual personal perspectives, our professional expertise, and our knowledge of the online environment, to provide parents and carers with the information and tools they need to help boys and young men resist and debunk misogynistic narratives. We are determined to push for a future where every boy grows up feeling he is 'man enough', without needing to adopt the restrictive and damaging model of masculinity promoted by Tate and his imitators.

We do not claim to be perfect parents. In fact, Amelia has reflections aplenty on what she could have done better raising her son, and Matteo struggles every day to balance online safety with responsible internet use for his young kids. We can both strongly relate to the many thousands of parents who fear losing their sons to the darker corners of the internet. But in the pages that follow, we'd like to offer up what we can of our own experience and skills to give readers the ammunition they need to take down the toxic manosphere once and for all.

We'll aim to do this by setting out the context of boys' wider lives. We'll take a look at some recent data, to get behind the alarming headlines and find out how boys are really doing out there in the world. What are the current trends in education, media consumption, mental health and political attitudes that are affecting them? We want to go beyond the 'moral panic' that sometimes goes hand in hand with concerns around boys' online radicalisation. We think it's only by acknowledging and addressing the real problems they are facing – from loneliness to lack of body confidence, social anxiety and academic underperformance – that we can prevent their grievances being weaponised by the forces of misogyny.

We'll go on to situate the manosphere phenomenon firmly in its wider social environment. Misogyny is not some new internet fad driven by influencers on TikTok. It is centuries old and embedded into many of the structures, institutions and traditions that rule our lives. The manosphere is merely the latest manifestation of the hatred and discrimination that has been directed at women, LGBTQI+ and gender-nonconforming people over human history. We'll take a look back at how and why these attitudes took root, how they show up in our lives today, and what we can do, in our own families, to push back against harmful and restrictive attitudes and practices. We are convinced that tackling misogyny at source, understanding the barriers and victimisation that women still face, and ensuring children do too, is key to raising men who respect and value women, not just online, but in real life too.

We want to challenge the idea that when women win, men lose. We think that explaining to boys that the goal of women's equality is not to oppress them, but to allow boys and girls the freedom to be who they want to be, will help them critically analyse the manipulation of 'masculinity' influencers. We'll take a look at how boys and men themselves may also be constrained by patriarchal narratives, such as the ideas often promoted by misogynists that they are valued only for their physical strength or financial success.

Then we'll trace the tangled history of the present-day landscape of the manosphere: in reality a complex network of overlapping sub-communities, influencers, public figures, forums and social media accounts that work in concert with unregulated algorithms to flood boys' content feeds with unrealistic portrayals of manhood and women-blaming storytelling. We'll show how earlier anti-feminist narratives sowed the seeds for the current crop of vile 'manfluencers' clogging boys' social media feeds.

We'll examine, in depth, the current media environment where young people are spending more and more of their time – one where young internet users appear to be showing a growing reluctance to engage with those whose views differ from their own, or to consume news content that challenges their political world views. This tendency is contributing to the formation of ever narrower digital echo chambers where, for boys, extreme misogynist content is becoming unavoidable. Taking a detailed look at some of the most popular influencers of the manosphere, each with millions of followers, we'll show how they reinforce narratives of traditional male dominance and aggression. We'll look at how these figures manipulate and monetise algorithms which lead boys quickly from content exploring valid interests in gaming, fitness and personal development to sexist stereotypes and outright misogyny.

We have also included the voices of young people themselves: boys *and* girls. Chapters Four and Five are devoted to hearing their views on the digital reality of their lives today, and the impact on them of online misogyny. In Chapter Six, we'll hear the sobering reflections of Calum, a remarkable young man who descended into the depths of the manosphere's rabbit hole, and managed to drag himself out again. Calum is now devoted to the cause of warning other young men away from the promise-strewn path of misogynistic influencers, who claim they offer a route to status and success. In reality, it is one founded on the debasement and humiliation of women, leading boys to nothing more than further isolation and alienation.

Despite the concerning nature of much of what this book will uncover about the content our boys encounter online, neither of us wishes to demonise technology. We are both 'very online' people, who spend our professional lives immersed in digital tech. We totally acknowledge the value of internet use – whether for education, learning or connection. Our aim is to adopt a realistic approach that will help parents prepare their boys for thoughtful, critical and responsible digital engagement. We think that, even with a child social media ban in place, until platforms adopt a safety by design approach to their products and features (and we may be waiting a long time for this), some risk is unavoidable. One recent study found that as many as 60 per cent of children were evading the ban in Australia.[9] Building kids' understanding of and resilience to digital dangers is key. Much as in the real world, a zebra crossing may exist to protect children from being run over, but they still need to stay alert and check for traffic before they cross the road.

In the final chapters of this book, we want to look to the future and offer parents what we hope are some useful tools and suggestions for inoculating boys against these hateful attitudes. We want to highlight the vital importance of fostering healthy and respectful family conversations, and consider how parenting norms need to adapt and evolve for the digital age. We will guide you through some of the techniques we use in our work to develop children's critical thinking and empathy. We believe these tools can easily be adopted by every parent to mitigate the impact of the torrent of toxic online hate. This is vital in a context where boys' consumption of online misogyny is not only powering hate towards real women and girls, but worsening their own mental and physical health too.

We will offer our thoughts on how to increase the chances that boys will open up to you and share their anxieties and concerns in the first place – a vital first step to kick-start supportive conversations. We've combined classic communication techniques with our own expertise in countering extremism to propose a unique blended approach to talking to boys about misogyny without immediately putting them on the defensive. The aim is to move these conversations away from panic and blame and towards active listening, empathy and collaborative problem solving. We'll offer our own hard-won tips, and, yes, we'll even cover the 'porn chat' that every parent dreads.

Our aim in writing this book is to leave you, our readers, as parents and carers, with a toolkit to protect the boys in your life from indoctrination by this hateful ideology. We hope that by doing so, we'll be contributing to the final demise of the ghastly manosphere and ensuring a safer, happier future for all of us, women and men, girls and boys. As a first step on the way to doing so, let's next take a closer look at the current state of British boyhood.

PART ONE
DIAGNOSIS

Chapter 1

Boys are Not the Problem!

Some of the most charming and timeless heroes in the history of storytelling have been boys. Boys, and the mischief and adventures that are assumed to follow them, have loomed large in our culture for centuries. Whether it's Bart Simpson, Dennis the Menace, Dustin, Mike and the D&D crew from *Stranger Things* or Harry Potter, we each have our own favourite fictional boy, usually characterised by a mix of bravery, risk-taking, confidence, kindness and a willingness to flout authority in the name of truth, justice or even just a good prank.

We are conjuring up for you the popular image of boyhood drawn from our shared culture because, for the last few years at least, boys' reputation has taken a bit of a dive in our national imagination. Whether it is in the news headlines, the speeches of politicians and experts, or, of course, the social media networks on which most of us spend at least some of our time, often boys are presented as a series of problems that need to be solved.

Let's brace ourselves to take a look at some of those recent shocking news stories from 2024 and 2025. This period included the arrest of 147 children, the vast majority of whom were boys, in riots following the murders in Southport of Elsie Dot Stancombe, seven, Bebe King, six, and Alice da Silva Aguiar, nine. The girls' murderer was himself only a boy – seventeen – at the time of the attack.[1]

Contributors to the website Everyone's Invited, where girls post about their experiences of sexual assault and 'rape culture' in school, have shared stories of being abused by boys, even in primary school. And teaching unions also warned that female teachers were raising the alarm about a rapid increase in misogynistic attitudes among boys.[2]

Over the past few years, we've seen growing evidence of boys' underachievement in education, a much discussed epidemic of loneliness, a higher proportion of men than women among young people not in education, employment or training, and a stark rise in violence against women and girls, including in schools.[3] It all paints a rather depressing picture of boys' place in British society. And it's a long way from the heroic and cheeky antics of the boys we love to read about and watch on screen.

This climate of anxiety about a crisis of 'toxic masculinity' among our boys reached its peak in March 2025, when Netflix screened *Adolescence*, a drama series that told the story of Jamie, a thirteen-year-old boy radicalised by online 'incel' ideology into a hatred of women and extreme violence. The series was critically acclaimed, particularly for the powerful performance as Jamie by young actor Owen Cooper, and within a week became Netflix's most streamed show in the UK. The drama clearly touched a national nerve, with much of the media coverage focusing on the fact that, for many parents, this may have been the first they had heard of the influence on their sons of shadowy online misogynists like Andrew Tate.

Press headlines screamed the alarm: 'Is this the most terrifying TV show of our times?' asked the *Guardian*.[4] Jess Phillips, safeguarding minister at the time, described *Adolescence* as 'a disturbing glimpse into the minds of thousands of young British boys warped by the extreme violence and sexual abuse they are witnessing every day online'.[5] Prime Minister Keir Starmer confessed that he found the series 'really hard to watch', and hosted a reception at Downing Street for its creators and relevant children's charities. He also encouraged teachers to show the series in schools and acknowledged parents' concerns about the issues it raised, while warning: 'There isn't an obvious policy response which will answer all of these questions.'[6]

Hot on the heels of *Adolescence* came the BBC's 2025 Richard Dimbleby Lecture, which was given by the former manager of England's men's football team, Gareth Southgate. In a passionate speech, Southgate described a generation struggling to find their place in society and lacking real-world opportunities for meaningful social connection and positive male role models.

He warned of the sinister voices of the online manosphere, who he claimed were denigrating women and promoting damaging stereotypes of masculine success to boys.[7]

Southgate's speech drew on a new report, *Lost Boys: State of the Nation* by the Centre for Social Justice – also widely covered in the media. Journalists seized on the headline statistic that more UK boys owned a smartphone than lived with their father, but the *Lost Boys'* in-depth findings went beyond fears of this 'epidemic of fatherlessness' to paint a worrying picture.[8] The research pointed to a generation of boys and young men lacking purpose and guidance, feeling lonely, underperforming in school and in work, and becoming more and more emboldened by the messages they receive via social media to blame these problems in their lives on women.

The report cited one survey for International Women's Day 2024 which found that 59 per cent of UK men (aged sixteen to seventy-four) somewhat or strongly agreed with the statement 'We have gone so far in promoting women's equality that we are discriminating against men.' Performing less well academically than girls, increasingly likely to be out-earned in their future workplaces, and receiving negative messages about 'toxic masculinity' from the adult world, some boys appeared to be seeking validation from the internet.[9]

One danger with this is that, now the vast majority of over-eights own a smartphone, normal teenage information-seeking behaviour, driven by curiosity about sex and relationships, can be rapidly funnelled online into the viewing, which may become compulsive, of more and more extreme content.[10] Children's viewing of pornography, which has become incredibly common, has undoubtedly triggered the most alarm among parents. The Online Safety Act's enforcement of age verification for adult websites has addressed this directly. However, the Children's Commissioner, Dame Rachel de Souza, reported in 2025 that many of these views are driven algorithmically on social media, rather than sought out by children themselves on dedicated porn sites.[11]

Since much porn is violent in nature (as much as 35–45 per cent of scenes in one recent study of 4,000 scenes from mainstream porn sites), its routine viewing by kids has been linked to the rise in sexual harassment and abuse in schools, and the adoption of increasingly risky sexual practices, such as strangulation, among young adults.[12]

The authors of the *Lost Boys* report also noted the emerging political divide between young men and women, with women becoming more progressive and left-leaning in their views while young men turn towards conservative or right-wing movements. They attributed this, at least in part, to online echo chambers, noting: 'In an increasingly online existence, boys and girls no longer walk the same path from childhood to adulthood, with their interests, values and aims in life increasingly incompatible with each other.'[13]

Data from 2024 on young people's attitudes to gender equality has confirmed significant gaps, finding that among sixteen- to twenty-nine-year-olds, 16 per cent of men agreed with the statement that 'feminism has done more harm than good', compared with 9 per cent of women. While the vast majority of men who had heard Andrew Tate's statements found them offensive, 20 per cent of this younger group did not – more than double the proportion of men aged thirty to fifty-nine. The same study found that women aged sixteen to twenty-nine were especially likely to say it is harder to be a woman, with 68 per cent feeling this way, compared with 35 per cent of men of the same age.[14]

There is a lot to unpick here, but what's crucial for us to note up front is that we don't think boys themselves are to blame for any of the trends we have explored in this chapter. If boys seem to be failing to maximise their possibilities for happiness and meaningful connection, surely that is our collective responsibility? We think that the adults in society, particularly those with the power to make changes, need to take a serious look at why this is the case and tackle some of the issues in society which have allowed this situation to arise in the first place.

But where does that leave us, as parents and carers? Is there anything we can do to improve the lives of our boys in the face of some pretty complex problems? The answer is yes. But first of all, a warning:

WARNING

We apologise in advance for the next couple of chapters, which will make for hard reading at times. But the fact is, it's only by properly diving into the *reasons* boys are getting sucked into the influence of online misogyny that we can take concrete action to tackle it. We want to go behind the headlines to uncover why these damaging narratives capture boys' attention. That means looking at the bigger picture from history and in society which, at times, may make you feel a bit low or helpless. But, we know, from our own work, that we can all do our bit to change things, and once we've laid out the foundations that misogynist influencers are building on, we'll show you the tools which will undermine them.

As parents ourselves we are also worried by everything we've drawn your attention to so far in this chapter. Like you, however, we also know and meet many boys and young men who are leading happy, engaged and productive lives. When we visit schools for our work with Shout Out UK, they talk to us about their hopes for the future and their frustration about the negative way they are sometimes perceived. And we all know, from our own families, how loving, kind and in need of affection and reassurance boys can be.

The evidence for a crisis of misogyny among boys is also nuanced. A recent YouGov survey, for example, found that only 7 per cent of thirteen- to seventeen-year-old boys had a favourable view of Andrew Tate and only 12 per cent believed that women had it better than men in today's society, comparing favourably with millennial men at 28 per cent.[15] Boys' views reflect a diversity of opinion which we don't always see represented in the scare stories.

In this chapter, we will attempt to get to the bottom of what life is like for today's boys. We think there is much that is overlooked in the overheated media commentary on boys and misogyny. So, let's dig into the data behind the headlines to figure out the realities of daily life for boys and young men. In the classroom, on playing fields, hanging out with friends, at home and online, how do boys experience the world, and, just as importantly, how are these experiences being reflected back at them by the parents, teachers, figures from popular culture, and other adults whose decisions affect their lives?

Schooled in Failure

Let's start with school. It's where our boys spend most of their days after all. For at least the last twenty years, based on most measures of academic success, girls have been doing better than boys in the classroom. According to the Higher Education Policy Institute, boys lag behind girls at every stage, from reception to sixth form, and into higher education.[16]

This gender attainment gap starts young. Children's early development has long been recognised as centrally important to their future well-being and life chances. Recent data shows 'school readiness', a crucial development measure for reception children, stands at 75 per cent for girls but, strikingly, only 61 per cent for boys.[17] At eleven, boys fall well behind girls in expected attainment levels in reading and writing. In 2024–25 66 per cent of girls met the standard compared to 59 per cent of boys. Notably, at this stage, girls are a striking 12 per cent ahead of boys in writing ability.[18]

Boys themselves notice this difference: Amelia's son, PJ, often remarked during his school career that girls were just 'naturally' more studious and treated less strictly by teachers than boys. These attitudes may become self-perpetuating in boys' peer groups where boys often fear being bullied for being a 'nerd' if they appear too conscientious. One boy quoted in the *Lost Boys* report said: 'If you want to do something different at school here you get bullied ... Boys have a hard time with trying to give an image that fits in so you don't get bullied or hurt.'[19]

Girls' lead in education is naturally reflected in the balance of young people entering further and higher education. In 2022–3, 57 per cent of UK students at university were women, a trend that has been consistent over many years.[20] Boys and young men are also one and a half times as likely to be excluded from school and form the majority of sixteen- to twenty-four-year-olds not in employment, education or training.[21]

You might think there would be political impetus to address this persistent gender attainment gap, but this has not yet emerged as a priority for any UK government.[22] The Education Select Committee has expressed its intention to hold an inquiry into the issue of boys' educational underachievement, but, as of February 2026, this has yet to take place.

Having been systematically denied access to education for centuries, women's educational progress over the last half-century has been phenomenal. It's now completely normal to find female GPs, politicians, solicitors, dentists and accountants. And we've all become used to the media reports on GCSE and A level results days of girls doing better than boys in almost every measure, with accompanying photos of triumphant girls. In 2025, 73.6 per cent of GCSE entries from girls achieved a grade 4 or above in comparison with 67.5 per cent of entries from boys.[23] Interestingly, much of the media coverage surrounding that year's results concerned the fact that boys, for the first time in years, achieved more A or A* grades at A level than girls by the tiniest of margins (0.2 per cent). This commentary focused on the reasons why girls' attainment might have slipped and asked whether more needed to be done to support them.[24]

It's important to celebrate girls' achievement in the face of historic inequality, but alongside this progress, it seems that we may now just take it for granted that girls do better at school. But what exactly is this preconception based upon?

Decades' worth of research into the subject has found that neither sex is more intelligent than the other. A recent comprehensive review found 'there are no overall (average) differences between women and men in general intelligence'. It continued, however, to outline some genetic differences in cognitive abilities: men showed a slight advantage over women in maths and mechanical engineering; women had better memory and verbal skills. Boys also tend to develop language and communications skills later than girls: 70 per cent of late talkers are boys, and girls gain language faster and have larger vocabularies.[25]

These differences don't account for the wider picture of boys' underachievement. In his influential 2022 book, *Of Boys and Men*, British-born social scientist Richard V. Reeves, founder of the American Institute for Boys and Men, has argued that over the past few decades, trends in education have caused a 'feminisation' of the school environment which may have unintentionally disadvantaged boys. His research puts men's contemporary struggles in the context of broader social trends like the decline of heavy industry, alongside the rise of feminism, women's entry to the workplace, and the loss of traditional models of masculinity for men.

In addressing boys' academic underperformance Reeves notes the brain's gendered differences mentioned above, such as the fact that, in girls, the prefrontal cortex, which influences organisation and impulse control, matures up to two years earlier than in boys. He has argued the case for boys starting school a year later than girls to reduce this cognitive gap. He has also suggested that the modern education system, with a focus on project-based learning and continuous assessment, may be inherently more 'female-friendly' due to girls' earlier organisational brain development.[26]

Reeves has also highlighted the fact that the vast majority of teachers at every school stage are women. Education secretary Bridget Phillipson has recently argued that more male teachers are urgently needed to provide positive role models and improve boys' engagement with school.[27] The numbers here are striking. It's true that women make up over three-quarters of the teaching workforce in England. Only 35 per cent of secondary school teachers are men, a tiny 14 per cent in primary and nursery school, and 30 per cent of primary schools have no male teachers at all.[28]

Richard Reeves's views on boys' educational underachievement are quite controversial. Certainly, his proposed solutions would require a huge reorganisation of our education system. Research among teachers has confirmed that 81 per cent would like to see more men in education, but a large-scale recruitment drive encouraging male graduates into teaching would not see results for many years given the current numbers within the profession.[29]

Other analysis has found little evidence that boys learn better from male teachers, or that they would benefit from starting school later.[30] Interventions which *have* been found to help boys in school, and which make more sense to us, include peer mentoring, where older boys supported younger pupils; early literacy support to help with reading; involving parents, particularly dads, in their sons' schooling; and developing positive attitudes to boys among staff.[31]

Some experts maintain that boys tend to be 'relational' learners.[32] This means that their success at school is directly related to the quality of their relationships with their teachers – whatever their gender. Concerningly, one consequence of boys' increasing exposure to misogynist attitudes online appears to have been a deterioration of their relationships with women teachers, who feel demoralised and disrespected by boys expressing attitudes learned from influencers such as Tate in the classroom.[33]

It is understandable to respond with shock when boys repeat sexist talking points, and some of our own team have experienced this in the classroom. Our own research has also shown that teachers often don't feel confident discussing subjects that might be considered controversial.[34] And, in interviews conducted for this book, some young people reported that conversations about masculinity influencers were shut down by teachers concerned about online misogyny. This risks fuelling boys' views that they are not listened to, or their concerns taken seriously, by the adults in their lives.

A 2025 report into teachers' perceptions of boys found that when they did engage directly in classroom conversations about masculinity, boys actually showed a wide range of attitudes to influencers such as Tate. Some challenged his views; others adopted his talking points and signature hand signals in school just to provoke and shock teachers and other kids, rather than because they fully signed up to his views. In direct chats with boys, teachers found that their feelings about masculinity were closely linked to a broader sense of their identity and their place in the world, which in turn affected not just their success in school, but their overall mental health.[35]

Hearteningly, the Department for Education's new guidance for schools on educating children about misogyny has specifically emphasised the importance of avoiding 'stigmatising boys for being boys' – a positive step.[36] However, when reflecting on all of the above, it is hard to resist the conclusion that, for many boys, school is an environment where the vast majority of authority figures are women, where they see girls as more successful at every stage of learning, and where their very masculinity may be framed as a problem. This situation is emphatically not teachers' fault – resulting as it does from a complex interplay of factors – but it can help us understand why boys may be susceptible to online grievance rhetoric.

Boyz (Not) in the Hood

Let's return to our fictional boys for a moment: the *Stranger Things* D&D crew braving the 'Upside Down' to save their town, Harry Potter riding pillion on Hagrid's motorbike to escape the repressive world of Privet Drive, and Bart Simpson rampaging unsupervised through the Springfield neighbourhood. Boys' stories often follow the hero's journey plot arc, where a young protagonist strikes out on an adventure, facing hazards along the way, which they ultimately overcome in a quest for greater wisdom and fulfilment (well, maybe not always in Bart Simpson's case). We often associate stereotypical boy pursuits with the outdoors: ball sports, climbing trees, fishing and making dens, or, in urban settings, hanging out at the local rec or sports ground. This popular idea of boys as rough and tumble physical adventurers, however, is far removed from the reality of modern boys' lives.

The benefits of physical activity have been clearly established for all children, with some research suggesting that they may be particularly important for boys. Certainly, taking part in sport and PE consistently emerge as among boys' most positive experiences of school, and an important way for teachers to keep them engaged.[37]

But sadly, kids' activity levels are in drastic decline. In 2024, only 49.1 per cent of children aged five to sixteen were active for an hour or more each day, with older teens, including boys, the least active school-age demographic.[38] From primary school, boys are more likely than girls to be obese.[39] Boys who don't live with their father appear to be at particular risk of obesity, reflecting, perhaps, the time-poor lives of single mothers as much as the lack of a dad to drag kids out to the park.[40] There is some evidence, though, that boys with fathers at home are more likely to be introduced to sport and to have the habit of physical activity instilled in them at a young age.[41]

In England, children's time playing outdoors has declined by 50 per cent in a generation, with fewer than three in ten children saying they play on their street.[42] Over four generations in one family, the distance eight-year-olds were allowed to roam unsupervised declined from six miles to just 300 yards.[43]

And there are plenty of external barriers to kids' play. Public spending on play facilities and annual parks' budgets have plummeted.[44] It's the same story of massive public underinvestment for youth centres, leisure centres and public sports grounds where boys and young men might once have spent time socialising and engaging in physical exercise. In the last twenty years, hundreds of youth clubs and playgrounds have closed.[45]

This reduction in outdoor play and physical exercise among children was compounded in 2020–1 by school closures and Covid lockdowns, which restricted children's outdoor lives even further. As the parent of a teenager at the time, Amelia saw her son's social life move from mostly outside the home – at school and extra-curricular activities like tennis and drama group – to entirely online.

The social psychologist Jonathan Haidt has mapped out a theory that the arrival of smartphones, combined with a parenting style that is more physically protective of children than in previous generations, has shifted childhood from 'play-based childhood' to 'phone-based'.[46] The pandemic appears to have turbo-charged trends that had already begun with kids' ownership of mobile phones.

For many boys, the sense of risk-taking and adventure that comes with outdoor physical play is now mostly found in online gaming. Girls, of course, also game, but boys are much more likely to play multiplayer console games, and to play violent shooter games. The evidence that playing violent video games may have an effect on boys' behaviour or attitudes in real life is not, in our opinion, convincing. But, as we'll look at later in the book, there is documented proof that many online gaming spaces are rife with hate speech and abuse.[47] It is this, we'd venture, rather than the games themselves that should be a cause for concern.

The anonymity of gaming platforms, as elsewhere on the internet, emboldens some players to use language they wouldn't in a face-to-face setting, and this might desensitise children to its harmful effects on others. The nature of online gaming is highly competitive and stressful – and we've both experienced this: Matteo as a committed gamer himself and Amelia as a mum concerned about her gamer son's mood swings as he yells at the other players on-screen. Sadly, this atmosphere can escalate into toxic behaviour and hate speech, often as a form of trolling or to vent frustration.

There are also some serious child safety concerns when it comes to gaming. Roblox, for example, is one of the most popular online games for children with a staggering 85 million daily active users globally, 14 per cent of whom are under thirteen. In 2025, it faced calls to implement stricter safety measures following an investigation which highlighted flaws in its age verification systems allowing adult strangers to communicate with children and children to access age-inappropriate content.[48] There is plenty of evidence that extremists, including misogynists, are using gaming spaces to recruit boys and young men, a theme we will revisit.

Boys also appear to be most at risk of becoming addicted to video games to the detriment of their mental and physical health. In 2022, nearly 90 per cent of users of the National Centre for Gaming Disorder's services were male.[49]

In his writings, Haidt has suggested that boys are inclined to seek out a degree of physical risk, a normal development for all kids in the transition from adolescence to adulthood. They need real-life experiences and setbacks, he maintains, to grow in self-reliance and maturity. He suggests that for boys, spending most of their time online is robbing them of these vital opportunities. Their retreat into a virtual world is fostering a sense of isolation and limiting their chances to develop social skills, manage anxieties and form stable relationships.[50] Most troubling of all, this online isolation, combined with the search for identity and independence which is intrinsic to being a teenager, may open boys up to some very disturbing influences indeed.

The New Battle of the Sexes

This decline of real-world opportunities for social connection among young people has sparked concern around the world. When he visited the UK in 2024, the former US surgeon general Vivek Murthy held a discussion with students and remarked afterwards: 'It became clear ... that their comfort with in-person interaction is diminishing over time, as we have less and less of it. In that regard our ability to interact with one another and build relationships is diminishing. That's our social muscle and like any other muscles we don't use it, it gets weaker.'[51]

The top four ways modern kids spend their spare time outside school are screen-based: watching streamed video content; using their phones to communicate with friends; watching TV and playing video games.[52]

For complex reasons, whether as a result of the impact of price rises, behaviour adopted during lockdown, a lack of spaces where they can freely socialise, or parental over-protectiveness, teenagers do appear to be meeting up less in person.[53] We both hung out with the opposite sex at youth clubs and town centres as teens, but now young people have fewer opportunities for meaningful leisure-time interactions with the opposite sex. We'd argue this may make boys more susceptible to some of the misogynist or heavily stereotyped gender narratives that they encounter online.

We hope that by this point, our summary of the challenges facing boys and young men today has given some explanation for why they may have some legitimate worries about their place in the world. The reason we are writing this book is because certain noisy online voices appear to be succeeding in converting this anxiety into misogyny, resulting in increasing harm to women and girls and what appears to be an uptick in hostility between the sexes.

Author and educator Laura Bates has spent many years campaigning for women's equality and visiting schools to talk to young people about sexism and misogyny. In her recent book, *Men Who Hate Women*, she notes the point, somewhere around 2017, that boys' responses to her talks in school began to change. She had experienced defensiveness, and even hostility, in their reactions previously, but she began to notice boys using the same talking points again and again: citing false or misleading statistics about rape and sexual harassment, for example, and echoing similar words and phrases such as, 'feminism is cancer'.[54]

This is a trend we've also noticed in our work in schools at Shout Out UK; being from two different generations ourselves, we do feel it marks a shift from our own younger years. Matteo's generation, the millennials, seemed to be at the forefront of efforts to forge a new model of gender equality, prepared to share housework and childcare with their partners and encouraging each other to call out sexism.

As we said above, the reality of boys' attitudes to girls and women is more nuanced than some alarmist headlines would lead you to believe, but there does seem to be a growing gender divide in popular online culture. We've seen young women alluding to this on social media lately, with some claiming they prefer to date older men as a result. One recent article quotes a nineteen-year-old woman saying of her millennial boyfriend: '(He's) a feminist – and weirdly, so are most of his mates. He missed all the manosphere stuff and it shows.'[55]

In some cases, young women are reacting to this backlash with rhetoric which is itself actively divisive. In 2024, aspiring comedian Megan Boni went viral on TikTok declaring: 'I'm looking for a man in finance with a trust fund, 6'5", blue eyes.' Although it was a joke about a shallow woman with a ludicrous 'shopping list' for a partner, perhaps it could also be seen as a message to men that anyone who didn't fit this description was not worth dating (another TikTok commentator estimated the number of single men in the US who might fit the bill: two.)

Adolescence is naturally a time for exploring your identity, including feelings around sex, sexuality and romantic relationships. Depending on the openness of the environments they were brought up in, previous generations may have learned about sex from their parents, siblings, at school or from their peer group. Recent research has revealed that children are now receiving their first information about sex and sexual relationships from the internet. And that 'information' is likely to be pornography. The Children's Commissioner's 2025 report found that the average age at which kids see online porn is now thirteen. Over a quarter of children surveyed had seen it by age eleven, and 73 per cent of all boys had seen it. Most children are not seeking this content out, it is being served to them algorithmically on their social media feeds, most frequently on X, but also on Snapchat, Instagram, TikTok and YouTube. Dame Rachel de Souza described social media sites as the 'gateways to pornography'.

Children themselves are expressing concern that they are learning sex from porn, and that since much of the pornography they see depicts the degradation of women or violence against them, this is affecting boys' attitudes to girls and women in the real world; 73 per cent of children, and 77 per cent of girls surveyed for the report agreed that viewing online porn affects young people's behaviour towards one another. One sixteen-year-old girl commented: 'It's too fake and can be violent, which is not good for boys, seeing that and thinking that's how they treat girls,' with another seventeen-year-old noting: '[Porn] makes boys act vile towards girls.' Other responses mentioned the impact on boys' self-esteem of porn by creating the misconception that being in a sexual relationship requires a man to be hyper-masculine and physically dominant: 'The boys could have seen that on porn and might be like, "Oh, I'm expected to do that." And then the girl might not want that and then it creates a whole [...] situation that could have been avoided.'[56]

The unhealthy depiction of sex and misogynistic attitudes on display in porn are present across some other online spaces inhabited by boys and men. At a time when boys may be making their first attempts at asking a girl out and dating, they are simultaneously bombarded online with misleading information about how, in modern heterosexual relationships, and the wider world in general, women are unjustly holding power over men. We can see why this might resonate with boys and young men who have lived through an isolating lockdown, had fewer opportunities to form strong real-world relationships and are likely to feel physically and financially inadequate when they compare themselves to the filtered and fake norms of the rich, ripped men they see on social media.

A poll carried out in 2025 found 53 per cent of men aged sixteen to twenty-four agreed with the statement that 'the majority of women are only attracted to a small subset of men'.[57] They were also more likely than other age groups to believe that women prioritise attractiveness and financial status when searching for a partner. In fact, those women aged sixteen to twenty-four who responded *actually* ranked a sense of humour, kindness and communication as their most valued qualities.

Another recent example of the common men vs women narratives which populate online youth culture is the controversy surrounding the second most popular app in the US in 2025, Tea, an app used by women to 'dish the tea' on men they have dated whose questionable behaviour has prompted them to warn away other women. With six in ten women in the US feeling dating apps are unsafe, Tea was developed from a desire to protect each other's safety, but it also faced criticism for accusing men without any recourse or due process. A spokesperson for Men's Health charity Movember noted that, for some men, it may validate the idea spread by masculinity influencers that women are 'out to get you'.[58]

Copycat gender-flipped apps quickly emerged in retaliation, seized on by misogynists, who rated women with derogatory language. In 2025, a data breach of Tea on Her saw personal information of 70,000 women leaked online. Misogynist communities on 4Chan and TikTok subsequently engaged in a campaign of frenzied doxxing* and harassment of users they had identified.[59]

In an adult world where it is still sadly too often taboo for men and boys to express their insecurities about sex and dating, the fake friends of what we now call the manosphere may offer easy (albeit false) answers to the questions most boys ask themselves at some point: 'Why won't she go out with me?', 'What if I never have sex?', 'Am I too ugly to get a girlfriend?'

The boys Laura Bates was encountering in classrooms around the UK may have been early followers of these online influencers. As we've mentioned, her warning has been echoed by concerned teachers, educators and youth workers around the country, and in the international outcry caused by *Adolescence*. TV shows *EastEnders* and *Waterloo Road* have both also recently featured

* 'Doxxing' is the practice of sharing identifying personal information such as addresses online and encouraging real world harassment and abuse.

misogyny storylines. In response, the government's 2025 guidance for relationships and sex education (RSE) in schools includes tackling the topics of misogyny, incel culture and harassment. But how can we best approach these issues with our own sons at home?

If you are reading this book, we will assume that you are as troubled as we are by the rise of online misogyny and would like to do your bit to help the boys in your life resist it. We have good news for you: no boy is born a misogynist. Views that are harmful to women are taught to boys by our wider culture, with many drawn to such messaging because it cleverly exploits their vulnerabilities and their valid insecurities about becoming men.

As adults, it's time for us to hold a proper conversation among ourselves and with the next generation of young men; one which opens up a space for their anxieties to be heard and acknowledges their challenges, rather than just telling them to 'man up'. We need to resist fatalistic narratives which stigmatise boys en masse as 'toxic' and reclaim the right for them to inhabit whichever version of healthy masculinity suits them best: queer or straight, jock or nerd, bossy or sensitive, dreamy or ambitious. Whatever combination of the above they may choose to be, our boys should consider themselves 'man enough'.

In the chapters that follow, we will look at some of the most promising approaches to help our boys. But first of all, let's take a step back to look at the big picture of misogyny in society. Because if misogyny is the enemy, we need to know where it came from, and how it shows up in our lives today to work out how to undermine it.

To help us, we are going to turn to an icon of femininity, rather than masculinity: Barbie.

Chapter 2

The Invisible System

In 2023, *Barbie* was a cinematic sensation. The highest-grossing film of the year, it made nearly $1.5 billion worldwide (the most successful film ever directed by a woman), and was nominated for dozens of awards. A multimillion-dollar marketing campaign made the film inescapable as brand after brand got onboard its hype machine with tie-in activity: clothing and make-up lines, video game product placement, even a real-life Barbie Dreamhouse in Malibu, California. Girls and women queued at cinemas to take selfies in 'Barbie boxes' before seeing the film.[1]

But the film also sparked a strong backlash from some prominent men who found it 'anti-men'. US political commentator Ben Shapiro posted a forty-three-minute denunciation of the film on YouTube, which opened with him burning Barbie, and her male sidekick, Ken, in a trash can.

Before we can begin to suggest how we inoculate the boys and young men in our lives against some of the hateful and women-blaming messages that they are likely to encounter online, we need to zoom out to look at the origins of these attitudes. We're going to ask you, as parents and carers of boys, to consider the nature of misogyny in our wider society, where it came from and how we might all, in fact, be susceptible to its influence.

Spoiler alert: if you've not seen it, this chapter will use the plot of the Barbie movie to make some points. That's because it is a good example from recent popular culture of an attempt to critique what is known as 'patriarchy'. Patriarchy is a social structure, based on discrimination on gender lines (what we usually call 'sexism'), in which men tend to occupy a higher position of power or status across the domestic, public, political and economic spheres.

This system, in varying forms, has existed for centuries and across many different cultures, based on the understanding of gender values and roles within society. The assumption that these roles are fixed by nature lies behind many of the ways men and women are perceived, and, in turn, how they act and feel in daily life. We'd like to stress that just because patriarchy favours male power within homes, workplaces, economies and governments, this does not mean that men always benefit from this power. As we showed in the last chapter, young men and boys face many of their own challenges and problems.

In fact, in this chapter, we'll argue that sexist gender norms and the strict definition of masculinity that is allowed within patriarchy may actually be exacerbating some of men's and boys' problems, including poor mental health and body image, and loneliness. We will take a look at what we mean by 'patriarchy', as well as considering 'sexism' and 'misogyny', how they differ, and how their impact harms boys and men, as well as women.

The beginning of the Barbie movie depicts a world where women, the Barbies, hold most of the power, status and visibility. We see a woman president and exclusively female doctors, pilots, politicians and lawyers; women, in fact, controlling all aspects of public and private life, with men, the Kens, occupying a supportive and largely decorative role. The plot of the movie involves Stereotypical Barbie (played by Margot Robbie) and Beach Ken (played by Ryan Gosling) travelling to the real world (our own) where they discover the existence of a world in which men are, by contrast, more dominant than women.

The film's opening scenes make visible something we take for granted, to the extent that it is usually largely hidden: even today, when women in our own world have made huge strides in achieving equality with men, they remain what the early feminist Simone de Beauvoir called, in her book of the same name, the second sex. Sadly, women are still disproportionately affected by discrimination, harassment and violence purely because of their gender.

The World Economic Forum reported in 2025 that, globally, based on current progress, women's earnings will continue to be, on average, lower than men's for the next 123 years.[2] Women continue to be under-represented in political leadership roles, making up only around a quarter of the world's parliamentarians and government ministers. In 2025, only sixteen women were heads of state. In the UK, the percentage of parliamentarians (MPs and peers) who are women is at a historically high level, but it is still far from parity at 36 per cent of the total.[3]

Violence against women is an international emergency: UN Women estimates that globally 'one in three women experience physical or sexual violence, most often by an intimate partner'. This statistic has remained largely unchanged for a decade.[4] The World Health Organization confirms that intimate partner violence is a major public health problem and a leading cause of injury and death for women worldwide.[5]

In *The Second Sex*, de Beauvoir argued that for too long men had considered themselves the default human beings, holding most of the power in the world, with their female companions relegated to a passive and supporting role. However, she argued that patriarchy may not necessarily be inevitable and natural, but based on social conditioning. That means that, as a society, we may reinforce gender roles by raising girls and boys differently and policing these roles strictly to make rebellion against them less likely.[6] Her book kick-started an argument over whether the origins of patriarchy lie in nature or nurture that still rages to this day.

Many people, such as the psychologist-turned-media commentator Jordan Peterson, continue to believe that it is a natural phenomenon, based on biological differences such as men's physical strength and greater aggression.[7] Recent research, however, suggests a more nuanced picture.

In his bestselling book, *Sapiens*, the historian Yuval Noah Harari finds the historical dominance of patriarchal power across societies 'bewildering'. He points out that physical strength is not a universal reason for holding and retaining power: the young are usually ruled over by older people; prominent leaders and politicians may be physically weaker than those they command. He also dismisses the idea that men's greater aggression explains their dominance. He asks, if aggression were the key to power, why would ruling women not simply put fierce male soldiers under the command of a more peaceful female government? Having considered the evidence, Harari confesses himself stumped, asking: 'If, as is being demonstrated today so clearly, the patriarchal system has been based on unfounded myths rather than biological facts, what accounts for the universality and stability of this system?'[8]

In her book *The Patriarchs*, the science writer Angela Saini addresses Harari's question. Drawing on research in archaeology, sociology, anthropology and genetics, she actually challenges the notion of patriarchy as an inevitable feature of human society. She argues that it may, in fact, be a relatively recent phenomenon in our history, and that gender inequality is rooted in culture rather than just biology.

She finds that patriarchy was not so widespread in early human societies, such as hunter-gatherer communities, where there is some evidence that men and women shared power. The rise of male domination may have been driven by the shift to settled farming in the Neolithic period, from which followed the concept of 'private property', requiring rules around inheritance and a stricter gender division of labour. Another possibility considered by archaeologists is that the large-scale Bronze Age migration into much of Eurasia of a more warrior-like population from what is now Ukraine and Russia entrenched more patriarchal ways of life.

Saini is sceptical of the idea that men's dominance is dictated by nature, providing examples of gender-balanced societies throughout history from what we know of life in the prehistoric city of Çatalhöyük in Turkey, to the Native American Haudenosaunee Confederacy, whose democratic society partly inspired the federal structure of the United States.[9]

Sexism: The Theory

Whether male dominance stems from biology or culture, or a mixture of both, its justification lies in sexism: the belief that a person's qualities and abilities are determined by their sex, with the assumption being, at least in the last few centuries, that women are inferior to men. Sexist ideas about men and women's natures, and the relative qualities and abilities of each, have dictated women's historically lower status in society. Whether in law, literature or customs, women have been considered not just physically weaker, but mentally inferior and of poorer character (hysterical, manipulative and promiscuous) than men. These attitudes are reinforced by most of the world's most influential texts, including religious scriptures.

The Bible, for example, contains many passages that are still used to justify women's subordination to men. Eve, the first woman, is an offshoot of Adam, created from his rib. She introduces sin to the world through her weak nature, succumbing to the temptation of the serpent and eating the forbidden fruit. For her weakness, she is punished with menstruation (still sometimes known as 'the curse'), childbirth and the command: 'Your desire shall be for your husband, and he will rule over you.' (Genesis 2–3.)

In the New Testament, the writings of Paul laid down strict gender rules which limited women's freedom of expression and participation in public life: 'Let a woman learn quietly with all submissiveness. I do not permit a woman to teach or to exercise authority over a man; rather, she is to remain quiet. For Adam was formed first, then Eve; and Adam was not deceived, but the woman was deceived and became a transgressor.' (1 Timothy 2:11–14.) Interestingly, the hierarchy of sexism here relates directly to women's moral failings, rather than to any intellectual or physical shortcomings.

Islam's foundational text, the Qu'ran, contrary to what is sometimes assumed by non-Muslims, holds that women and men share moral and spiritual parity. However, it also contains verses which enshrine the man's position as head of the household: the most cited verse on this topic is *Surah* An-Nisa (4.34), which states, 'Men are the protectors and maintainers of women, because Allah has given one more strength than the other, and because they support them from their means.'

Classical Greek thought, hugely influential in the development of Western societies, also offered many philosophical justifications for male dominance. Aristotle described women as 'deformed males', and argued that their biological inferiority made their submission to men both natural and necessary.[10] In Greek mythology too, Pandora, the first woman, opened the famous box which brought suffering and pain to humanity. This story, like that of Adam and Eve, casts a woman as the principal source of human troubles. This narrative repeats across many cultures and religions throughout the world.

Women have played important roles in society over these centuries of patriarchy, but history is, of course, largely written by those who hold the most power – in this case men – so much of their contribution has been written out of the textbooks.

For example, Matteo is a huge fan of the TV show *Vikings*, which features the character of Lagertha, wife of the legendary warrior Ragnar. According to the twelfth-century Danish historian

Saxo Grammaticus, Lagertha helped Ragnar reclaim his throne by leading women dressed as men into battle. The TV series has been attacked by men online for its unrealistic portrayal of women as warriors (relax guys: we can't know for sure whether either character actually even existed – historical retellings back then incorporated a fair dose of fantasy and allegory).

But these same men probably don't know of the warrior tomb in Birka, Sweden. Back in 1878, archaeologists discovered an impressive tenth-century tomb housing the remains of a Viking warrior, buried alongside a huge arsenal of weaponry and games of military strategy. They concluded this person must have been a prominent military general and experienced horseback archer. In 2017, DNA evidence showed conclusively that this richly commemorated warrior was also a woman.[11] Rather than rewriting history, the TV show may be more accurate than its detractors would like to believe.

Another example: think of a pirate. We are willing to bet the one that springs to mind will be 'Blackbeard' aka Edward Teach, the most notorious of them all. However, Zheng Yi Sao, a woman, commanded over 40,000 pirates during the height of her career in the nineteenth century.[12]

Sexism and the patriarchy helped build societies where women, until the last 150 years or so at least, were excluded from receiving an education, owning property, controlling their own bodies, or independently participating in social, political and financial activities such as voting, banking, and accessing legal services. Patriarchy became self-sustaining as women's lower levels of education and independence, and the cultural pressures to primarily involve themselves in nurturing children and catering domestically to men, left them without much agency to challenge the system.[13]

Nevertheless, with the advent of the feminist movements of the nineteenth and twentieth centuries and the resulting social upheaval, women and their male allies have forced change. In recent decades, the sexes have undoubtedly become more equal. Women in Western Europe, North America and many other places around the world have won the right to vote, to an education (where they are outperforming men, as we saw in Chapter One), marriage and property rights, equal parental rights and control over their reproductive lives. Women now participate in most aspects of public life and, in the UK, made up 48 per cent of the country's total workforce in 2025.[14] After long battles by campaigners, British women's equal rights are enshrined in law, specifically, the 2010 Equality Act, which offers legal protections at work, in education and in public services to anyone facing sexual discrimination.

In the eyes of the law, then, it is no longer acceptable in the UK, and in many other countries, to treat women less well than men. But every movement towards progress has historically faced a backlash. Sadly for all of us, as Barbie realised when she visited our world, the long journey to equality between the sexes is not over. The sexist attitudes that fuelled inequality for women persist, and may even be increasing. At this point in time, some men appear nostalgic for, to paraphrase *American Dad*, a 'better time' when men 'had all the power instead of just most of it'.

Misogyny: The Practice

In 2002, the OED's definition of misogyny as 'hatred of women' was broadened to 'hatred or dislike of, or prejudice against women'. This newer definition reflects the ways in which modern writers and thinkers have attempted to refocus thinking about misogyny away from the thoughts and actions of individual men who 'hate women' and towards the wider systems that sustain them.

The philosopher Kate Manne argues that misogyny is the '"law enforcement" branch' of sexism.[15] Its function is to control women, LGBTQI+ and non-binary people, using violence if necessary, and punish those who deviate from strict gender norms. If the sexist attitudes of a society dictate that women owe men certain domestic or sexual services, or must behave in a way men deem suitable, misogyny is the hostility faced by women who are perceived to fail in these duties.

The female dolls of Barbieland don't realise the power they hold in their own world until Barbie and Ken visit our own. There, Barbie responds with horror to the way she is treated. She is leered at, patronised and groped, and her shock makes more noticeable some of the things we often take for granted, like women being routinely catcalled by men in public.

You may be asking yourself what is the link between men leering at women as they pass on the street and the kind of radical and harmful misogyny which poisoned the mind of the child murderer, Jamie, in *Adolescence*? Well, although our news shows cover acts of violence against women and girls on a daily basis, these crimes are often depicted and discussed as the product of an individual man's psychological problems.

We have to assume that the majority of men do not commit violent acts against women, but some feminists have argued that until we recognise the sexism and misogyny ingrained in the broader social structures and thought patterns of our daily lives, we will never be able to eliminate the violence against women which is their horrific endpoint.[16]

The pyramid of misogyny is a tool developed by educators which we use in our anti-misogyny work at Shout Out UK. It illustrates how seemingly small 'microaggressions', such as sexist jokes at work or the belittlement of women in everyday conversations among men, exist on a continuum of a wider culture of misogyny.[17] These smaller acts build a wide base for the normalisation of gender discrimination, which culminates in violent crimes against women, such as stalking, sexual abuse and rape.

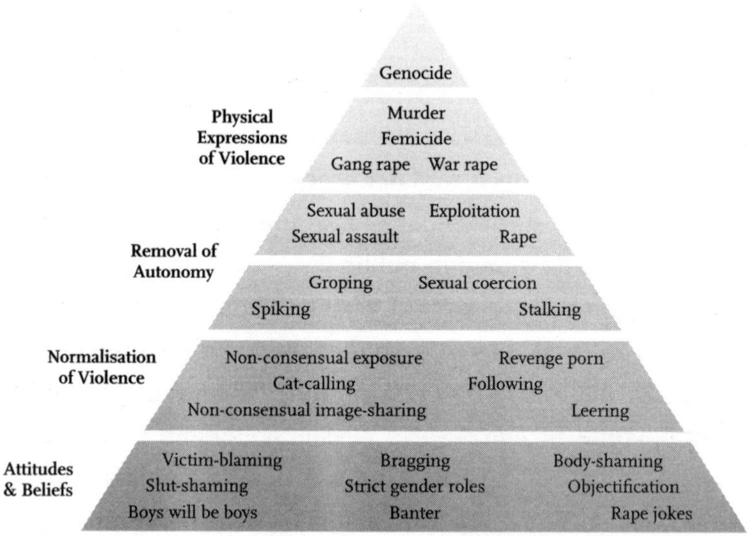

Adapted from: Sexual Assault Centre, University of Alberta

Far from the toxic reaches of the manosphere we worry about as parents, there are many mainstream institutions that hold huge power over our lives where gender inequality is still the norm. Recent investigations and inquiries in the UK have uncovered disturbing evidence of hostility to women, purely on the basis of their sex, in many public sector environments, institutions and workplaces.

In 2022, the Women and Equalities Committee of the UK Parliament found 'medical misogyny' entrenched in our health institutions, with women's symptoms often dismissed or minimised, sometimes leaving them in pain for years.[18] The British Medical Association acknowledged a 'culture of sexism' in a 2021 survey which revealed that 91 per cent of female doctors had experienced sexism in the past year.[19]

The Catholic Church has faced criticism for its continued exclusion of women from the priesthood and history of persecution of women facing unmarried motherhood. In 2021, the UK schools minister expressed 'serious concerns' about relationships and sex education in Roman Catholic schools, with teaching materials being used which could 'normalise non-consensual behaviour' and which warned girls that taking the contraceptive pill would harm them.[20]

Reports from Ofsted and the National Secular Society have also highlighted issues of sexism and gender discrimination in some Muslim schools, with schools segregating children, offering boys more opportunities and stocking library books with misogynistic content.[21] And of course, as we have already seen in previous chapters, sexual harassment and bullying appears to be rife in every kind of school. Girlguiding's 2025 annual Girls'

Attitudes Survey found that one in ten girls aged eleven to sixteen have missed school to avoid sexual harassment.[22] Ofsted's rapid review in 2021 found over a third of girls in mixed-sex schools had been harassed, and that sexual harassment was becoming 'normalised' for students.[23]

Our female politicians face not just obscene amounts of online trolling and abuse, but what has been described by Labour peer Harriet Harman as a 'climate of misogyny' within Parliament itself.[24] In a 2023 survey by the Fawcett Society, 69 per cent of women MPs reported witnessing sexist behaviour in Parliament, with one commenting: 'It's still an all-boys club ... and there is no leadership, either from Party hierarchy, leader of House, Prime Minister, Chief Whip ... no leadership shown from any of those individuals about how you crack down on sexism and harassment and abuse in this place – they would much rather sweep it under the carpet.'[25]

Recent examples which made press headlines include one male MP watching porn in the House of Commons and others claiming Angela Rayner, at the time the deputy leader for the opposition, was crossing her legs suggestively in Parliament to distract the prime minister.[26] Whistle-blowers have drawn attention to predatory behaviour, with sexual harassment frequently experienced by MPs and staffers, and ineffective disciplinary processes.[27] Sadly, this is a situation which will do little to increase women's participation in politics, where, as we have seen, they are under-represented.

In March 2023, the Baroness Casey Review found evidence of rampant sexism and misogyny in the Metropolitan Police. Commissioned following the murder of Sarah Everard by a serving police officer, the report detailed routine abuse of female members of staff, a culture in which 'predatory and unacceptable behaviour has been allowed to flourish' and where violence against women and girls was not taken as seriously as other forms of violence.

Examining incidents such as the handling of the murder of sisters Bibaa Henry and Nicole Smallman, where officers shared photos of the victims' bodies in WhatsApp groups, the report depressingly concluded that misogyny in the Met was 'systemic and fundamental' in nature.[28] This finding was reinforced by the activities and comments of officers seen in the 2025 BBC *Panorama* report, 'Undercover in the Police', which included expressing disbelief of victims reporting domestic violence.

In 2022, a 'cultural audit' of the British Army commissioned (and, it appears, subsequently kept quiet) by the Ministry of Defence uncovered a 'lad culture' fuelled by misogyny and 'enduring sexism', with sexual harassment of female soldiers and staff frequent.[29] It's hard not to conclude that this environment may have contributed to the tragic suicide of Royal Artillery gunner Jaysley Beck, who had faced a relentless campaign of unwanted sexual advances from a senior colleague, but felt she would be punished if she complained.[30]

Barbieland this is not.

In the BBC's coverage of Jaysley Beck's suicide, her persecutor, Bombardier Ryan Mason, is described as 'experiencing mental health issues at the time'. This is a good example of a media framing which places the blame squarely onto the individual man and his psychological struggles. He is, of course, entirely responsible for his own actions, but surely, we must also acknowledge the wider culture – the banter, acceptance of sexist stereotypes, and entitlement at the base of the pyramid of misogyny – which allowed his behaviour to flourish unchecked?

What are Little Boys (and Girls) Made Of?

The fact is, we all work together to sustain many of the cultural norms of a sexist society. And it does take work. The most up-to-date surveys of research on biological sex differences in the brains of men and women find widespread agreement that these differences are minor.[31] Despite the obvious physical differences of size, strength and reproductive organs in adult men and women, in terms of cognition, intelligence and emotional capacity, we are more alike than we are dissimilar. The neuroscientist Lise Eliot notes in her book *Pink Brain, Blue Brain*, that 'boys' and girls' brains are remarkably alike', though boys' brains are on average bigger than girls' (8–11 per cent). This size difference continues through to adulthood and is proportionate with males' bigger overall size in terms of both height and weight.[32]

And yet our own experience shows us that girls and boys *are* different. We have both observed this in our own kids and their friends: boys do seem to be more competitive, aggressive and physical, and girls more invested in their friendships, chatty and eager to please. Girls and boys talk, play, study and act so differently that we use many gendered descriptive terms quite naturally. 'Boys will be boys', of course, denotes that boys will tend to take risks and get into trouble; 'a bit of a lad' might be someone who is cheeky, a boozer or a womaniser; calling someone 'girly' might mean they love glittery clothes, romcoms and Taylor Swift, or of course, they might be a conscientious and studious 'girly swot'.

We all carry with us solid expectations of how we expect girls and boys to behave, even from early childhood, but the scientific evidence that all these behaviours are innate is slim. There are definite small differences in male and female brains which can be attributed to the influence of hormones while the foetus is developing in the womb, and later, during puberty and the onset of sexual impulses. However, the latest consensus among experts is that these small differences are amplified by the process of 'socialisation' we all undergo from the moment we are born.[33]

The difference in boy and girl babies' behaviour on gender lines is small. In fact, boy babies tend to cry more and need more comforting – contradicting the stereotype of boys as less emotional than girls.[34] Babies are, of course, unaware of gender. However, by the age of two, most children understand the two biological sexes and by three, know which they fall into. By the time children leave infant school at six, they have already grasped the behavioural norms of boys and girls, and are playing and communicating quite differently from each other. In *Delusions of Gender*, her landmark study of the science of sex differences, Cordelia Fine builds a persuasive case that biology alone cannot explain this shift, asking: 'Is it possible that parents' implicit attitudes about gender might be subtly transmitted to their children?'[35]

Fine and Eliot both propose that, rather than being hardwired naturally to behave as a boy or a girl, children are learning gender differences all the time: from their parents, from their family, their peers and from the culture and media around them, starting with the fairytales they listen to as toddlers and the cartoons they watch (Hello, Disney!).[36] Children's brains are incredibly malleable, and this neuroplasticity means that the more they are exposed to certain activities and tasks, the better at them they will ultimately become.[37] The heavy gendering of childhood that starts with different toys, differing depictions of the two sexes in books and games, even the contrasting ways adults speak to boys and girls, creates a kind of feedback loop where small initial sex biases are exaggerated and reinforced in children's own brains and by the world at large.[38]

So, for example, boys appear to show slightly more of an early preference for physical play than girls. This is then reinforced by their carers, with many studies showing that parents praise and overestimate boys' physical capabilities, starting with crawling and walking, making them more likely to encourage them in active play.[39] Boys subsequently spend more time playing sport, running, throwing and climbing, and may develop stronger spatial awareness skills as a result.[40]

As a general rule, girl children talk earlier than boys. This means that adults tend to engage in more verbal interactions with girls, using a wider vocabulary and greater nuance. As we saw in the last chapter, girls enter school with greater verbal skills and expression than boys, gaining a head start on boys in learning to read and write. There are small differences in boys' and girls' emotional processing: studies show that women appear to have a slightly higher propensity for empathy, with, for example, girl babies more responsive to changing facial expressions in adults.[41] Our society emphasises this tendency, alongside the biological fact of women's childbearing and lactation, as evidence of girls' intrinsic 'nurturing' nature, which then propels them towards taking on the lion's share of domestic labour and caring roles in families and communities.

As the movement for global gender equality has grown over the last fifty years, attitudes are slowly changing. One recent survey The Future is FeMale, of more than 12,000 people in thirty-two countries showed that 61 per cent of women and 46 per cent of men were in favour of children being raised in a more gender-neutral way.[42]

However, we do emphasise gender distinctions to our children – often unthinkingly. There is nothing at all wrong with dressing girls in pink skirts and buying boys toy diggers, of course, but these social factors may make each gender more likely to behave in ways that we think of as typical of their sex. That's not a problem when children are given the chance to express themselves how they choose. Matteo's daughter, for example, loves pink and has at least eight dolls, but she also loves muddy play outdoors and helping to prepare the barbecue. But when kids are forced into rigid stereotypes, it runs the risk of closing down their life choices and causing them harm. That's true of some of the sexist assumptions which affect women, and it can also have a crushing impact on boys and men.

Ken and the 'Man Box'

In the movie, Ken is very taken with our own world, where men appear to be in charge. He recognises that he and the other male dolls are not allowed full equality in Barbieland, so he decides to import patriarchy back there to give the men their turn. This goes well at first. The Barbies become brainwashed into the idea they are inferior and fall into line. Kens take over all the positions of power and the physical spaces of Barbieland which becomes 'Kendom'. Barbie's Dreamhouse becomes the hilarious, frat boy-themed 'Ken's mojo dojo casa house'. The female dolls cater to the men's needs and whims submissively, just as the Kens did for the Barbies earlier in the film.

Together with her human ally, Gloria, Barbie eventually succeeds in overthrowing this newly installed patriarchy. She ultimately manages to persuade Ken that he does not need to be dependent on her approval, but is an autonomous person in his own right, or 'Kenough'.[43] However, with a few concessions to the Kens, the female dolls appear to be pretty much restored to the complete power they held at the beginning of the film. The matriarchy of Barbieland lives on – presumably to be revisited in many lucrative sequels.

Sequels aside (and we'll be first in line for these), this felt like a missed opportunity to us. Is the choice facing us really between men dominating women or vice versa? Too often, this is how we see feminism falsely framed in the online content of the manosphere, which we'll look at in more detail in the chapters that follow. Influencers with millions of followers, such as the inevitable Andrew Tate and the British YouTuber Hamza, pose women's rights as an explicit threat to men, describing women as hell-bent on taking men's rights away from them and forcing them into a subordinate position in society.[44]

This is a wilful misinterpretation of the aims of feminism. The push for women's equality has never been about forcing men to take second place. In fact, by challenging the restrictive norms of patriarchy, such as that men must always bear total financial responsibility for the household and never show their emotional or physical vulnerability, many feminists have been at the forefront of advocating for women *and* men to have wider choices over how they live their lives. It's time to move beyond this battle of the sexes which pits men against women, and push back against the increasingly prevalent zero-sum idea that one sex must always lose out to the other.

Another arm of feminism has long considered how some of the traditional ideas and stereotypes of masculinity have limited men and boys. Equimundo, perhaps the leading global organisation researching men and gender equality, has enumerated the qualities that patriarchy demands of men. These include:

- Self-sufficiency, the idea that men must be completely independent, not relying on others and not needing to ask for help.
- Being tough. Men must be physically strong and emotionally stoical.
- Rigid gender roles and division of labour. Men must be the breadwinners outside the home with women taking on childcare and domestic responsibilities.
- Heterosexuality and homophobia. Real men only have sexual relationships with women and despise queer people.
- Aggression and control. Men must be prepared to use physical violence to gain respect, and maintain strict control over their wives, girlfriends and families.

We can easily recognise these traits as the stock-in-trade of popular online masculinity influencers such as Andrew Tate and British 'manfluencer', HS TikkyTokky. Equimundo uses the term 'man box' for this set of expectations on men, and they've amassed a lot of fascinating data on how boys and men really feel about life in and out of the 'man box' and how it affects their well-being. They have found that men's views on the expectations of traditional masculinity are complex, full of variation and contradiction, and there is definitive evidence over time that some are pushing back against the restrictions of the box.[45]

Men and women are generally becoming more in favour of shared household and childrearing tasks, and joint breadwinning, for example. A 2024 study found that the vast majority of those surveyed across twenty-four countries disagreed with the statement that 'A man who stays home to look after his children is less of a man.'[46]

However, with a new backdrop of the recent rise in online influencers glorifying traditional masculinity, we think it's important to consider other, more troubling tendencies. It appears that men who are most firmly inside the box, answering in favour of the need to control women and to show aggression to be respected, for example, are more likely to commit violence against women and to verbally and physically abuse women and queer people.

An Equimundo survey from 2017 of young men aged eighteen to thirty found that men aligned to 'man box' beliefs were up to six times more likely to report having bullied or assaulted other men and to report having committed sexual harassment. Adherence to these strict rules of masculinity also appears to have negative consequences for men's mental and physical health, with men in the box more likely to engage in dangerous health behaviours such as alcohol and drug abuse and unprotected sex, and more likely to meet the threshold to be considered depressed. They also ranked particularly highly for suicidal thoughts.[47]

These findings have recently been backed up by a 2025 study which compared the views of men who consumed content from influencers advocating for traditional masculinity with those of men who did not. The report linked engagement with such influencers to poorer mental health and risky physical health behaviours. Men who engaged with masculinity influencers were twice as likely as those who didn't to take steroids, and almost twice as likely to have taken testosterone injections.[48] Concerningly, more boys than ever are expressing anxieties about body image, perhaps as a result of pressure to have a ripped physique from fitness influencers, whose content often overlaps with the manosphere.[49]

The 'man box' is an unforgiving place for men seeking connection and support too. The idea that men must be self-sufficient and not show vulnerability or ask for help from others is most likely behind the recurrent statistic that men are more reluctant than women to visit a medical or mental health professional, with serious consequences for their health.[50] It is still considered less acceptable for men to show emotional distress (other than anger) than for women. In the words of Andrew Tate himself: 'You're not supposed to be happy. You're supposed to be monumentally influential and capable.'[51]

For boys and young men, who may be struggling with feelings of inadequacy or asking themselves valid questions about which qualities the world values, these messages have an impact, whether they realise it or not.

In her book, *The Will to Change*, the feminist author and activist bell hooks argued that the strict gender norms of patriarchy force men to suppress their emotions to the extent that they are denied the ability to fully love and be loved.[52] Faced from an early age with social conditioning that requires them to avoid expressing emotion for fear of ridicule, many men and boys disconnect from the openness and vulnerability needed in truly loving relationships, seeing it as weakness. This, combined with the idea that they must be able to solve their own problems, may leave them isolated and over-reliant on power and control over others. For parents of boys, who may be aware of some of the recent coverage of a 'loneliness epidemic' among young men, this is food for thought.[53]

Breaking Boys out of the Box

We believe that breaking down gender stereotypes and restrictive ideas about how each sex is supposed to look, love, work and behave in the world will benefit boys and men, just as much as girls and women. Trying to follow the model of masculinity promoted by 'manfluencers', which tells boys that their worth as a man is based on looks, money, hyper-heterosexuality and dominance, may inflate boys' feelings of superiority temporarily, but it will not help them long term with the disconnection and loneliness that is fuelling so much mental distress among young men.

Fifteen years' worth of data from Equimundo has found that men with less restrictive attitudes towards gender lead happier and healthier lives, with improved mental and physical health.[54]

These findings have been backed up by research showing convincingly that gender equality benefits everyone in society, not just women.[55] Freeing boys from rigid stereotypes opens up the world to them: it gives them the freedom to express their impulses to care and nurture which, in turn, may empower them to pursue careers in those traditionally female-dominated fields like nursing and education where more male role models are sorely needed. It gives them the opportunity, free from judgement, to take on a greater role in childcare and family life, improving their relationships with spouses and children. And by rejecting 'man box' stoicism and feeling comfortable expressing their feelings from boyhood onwards, men will ultimately have stronger mental health and be able to form more satisfying relationships with friends, family and intimate partners.

As we've shown, harmful gender stereotypes permeate the world at large, but there is lots we can do, as parents and carers, to resist them by modelling equality in our daily lives. Let's start with our own relationships. If we behave in respectful, egalitarian ways at home – within a heterosexual couple, for example – sharing chores and housework and taking an equal role in childcare, our children will grow up considering this the norm and be less likely to succumb to the 'make me a sandwich' rhetoric of misogynists who want to brand domestic labour entirely women's domain. Dads who pack school lunches and do the weekly washing are hardly thin on the ground these days, so let's make sure we are talking about and normalising this behaviour in front of boys. We are the first 'influencers' for our kids, after all.

We both grew up with fathers who had minimal emotional or domestic involvement with our day-to-day lives. For Matteo, this lack of a positive role model has made him determined to break the cycle and be more present for his kids than his own father was. Even in cases of parental separation or divorce, which is an unavoidable fact of life sometimes, boys (and girls!) benefit from dads who are physically present and emotionally available. Since much data shows that men increasingly want to play a major role in their children's lives, let's celebrate that fact. We could start by reforming paternity leave to give men more of a chance to bond with their children at the earliest stage, as some campaigners are pushing for.

If our kids grow up with a home life which is far removed from the controlling and unequal version we see trumpeted by the manosphere, they will be more likely to embark on healthy relationships themselves. If small boys are comforted by their parents and carers when they are upset or scared, rather than told to 'man up' or laughed at and shamed as a 'pussy' or the like, they may be more likely in adolescence to confess to feelings of depression and seek help, instead of becoming a tragic statistic.

If kids feel loved for themselves by their families whatever their sexuality and gender identity, rather than feeling they must fit into the heterosexual norm at all costs, they'll feel more resilient out in the world when they do inevitably encounter homophobia or transphobia.

Language matters, too. We can all make sure to use gender-inclusive language with our kids – 'police officer', for example, rather than 'police man' – so we are not implying that some roles in society are only open to one sex or the other. And family members of either sex can make sure to avoid using language which is derogatory, misogynist or blaming – 'slutty', for example, or 'bitchy'.

Through our professional practice at Shout Out UK we know that punitive approaches are less effective at changing behaviour than frequent small lessons and reminders. If you want to talk to boys about the reality of sexism and misogyny and their impact on women, you don't have to run them through the heavy data we've presented in this chapter; you can incorporate these ideas into everyday conversations on a daily basis. 'Luke's dad said he was playing like a girl at football practice. What do you think he meant by that?' might open up a discussion about what the use of 'girl' as an insult means about how men and women are perceived, and whether girls are naturally bad at sport (perhaps touching on the recent successes of England's women's rugby and football teams).

'Why do you think the girls at school are not allowed to wear trousers?' could be used to talk about how women's dress has often been policed by wider society, why this is the case and what it might mean for their freedom of expression.

'I overheard Dylan calling you gay for having a friend who is a girl. What do you think he meant by that? Why would he use that word?' might start a conversation about gender stereotypes, homophobia and the importance of mixed-sex friendships. We think it's important to listen carefully to boys' responses and not shame them if you don't like what they are saying. Instead gently question their assumptions – and your own. By doing so, you will model to them the vital critical-thinking skills and emotional resilience to resist those who tell them that one set of people is inferior to another based solely on whether they are a Barbie or a Ken.

And, of course, talking can only take us so far. Even more important, we think, is to model the behaviour and attitudes that we would like to pass on to our children. Mums can demonstrate to their sons, for example, how they value their financial independence, and dads can show them, through their actions, what an emotionally available and caring man looks like. This, more than the toys we buy for our kids or whether they prefer frilly dresses or football boots, will thwart the lies spread by the manosphere.

Speaking of which: brace yourselves; it's time to dive into its murky depths.

Chapter 3

The (M)analogue Beginning

We've now taken you through all the heavy context of why we find ourselves in the position of having to write this book. Misogyny is age-old and there's a backlash against the progress women have made; boys are struggling with valid problems in many areas and their insecurities and grievances are not being effectively tackled; bad actors are stepping into the void to promote an anti-women agenda. All this is having a real-world impact on young people, boys and girls. The way men and women are raised and conditioned along stereotypical gender lines is not helping. It's a lot to process while we wait for those *Barbie* sequels.

Although we think of it as a recent phenomenon, the rise of the manosphere has in fact been a long time coming. As a young(ish!) father, and a middle-aged mum, we each have our own perspective on the challenges this new world of online misogyny poses. However, as media literacy professionals, we are both aware of some of the rapid social and digital trends which have contributed to its spread. And Matteo, a millennial, had a ringside seat as a teenager as one of the first generations to come of age through this period of unprecedented transformation.

In this chapter, we will take a look at the roots of the enormous social and technological change which has facilitated the growth of the divisive misogynist rhetoric promoted by the likes of Andrew Tate. We will then take a trip down the rabbit hole to discover more about the present day manosphere: what is it, who are its main organisers, and how do they operate to influence boys and men? Most importantly, what are their true motivations for spreading this hate?

We both grew up with a very different media landscape from today. When Amelia was a kid, the internet did not even exist, though as a lifelong tech early adopter, she did have one of the first generation of home computers, the ZX81! Even during Matteo's childhood, the World Wide Web, as many people still called it, was not widely accessible. His life as a kid was rooted in the traditional play spaces of the offline world – parks, playgrounds and his own and friends' gardens.

As Matteo got a bit older, games consoles did become reasonably common. You may, like him, recall the old Nintendo 64 and PS2. But the computer games he and his friends played were mostly story-driven, single-player games. The few multiplayer games he knew (who remembers *GoldenEye 007* or *Mario Kart*?) were played together with friends at each other's houses – and video gaming was just one of many other real-world activities they did together, like football or judo. The opportunities for communication online with strangers were limited for most – not that Matteo's parents would have restricted him from doing this anyway, as, unlike today, there was no real discussion or media attention given to the dangers the internet might pose to kids.

Even once Matteo had his own home computer and games console at home, before mobile technology, the internet was still something that was restricted to the house. You had to be plugged into a computer and that device was, as likely as not, in a room where your parents might pop in at any moment. His both used a computer for work in the noughties, though they weren't exactly tech-savvy. In fact, like kids today, Matteo was often called upon as tech support since they didn't have a clue. Some things never change.

Secondary school for Matteo was the age of the flip phone, but interactions on these were limited to texting within friendship groups or attempting to record music to use as a ringtone. The same went for those early social media platforms like MSN and MySpace. Kids used them, sure, but primarily for communicating with people they knew in real life. There was also nothing at all which offered the seamlessly interactive features of, say, Instagram and TikTok today.

This was also true for the early file-sharing sites loved by teenagers in the 1990s and 2000s. These were commonly (and illicitly) used to access music and film, before they were largely shut down and, for the most part, everyone moved over to paid-for streaming services. Back then, in an age of dial-up broadband and limited bandwidth, kids had to actively research and understand how to perform tasks online to get what they wanted. Though Matteo found this frustrating at the time, looking back, he can see that children were forced to think critically to solve these problems. Online engagement was active and required some ingenuity. And of course, there was no danger of getting hooked into endless 'doom-scrolling' since the addictive technology of the 'feed' we know so well now from smartphones and social media did not exist.

For kids of the noughties, MSN Messenger was a game changer. This was the online space where you could spend entire evenings chatting to the people you'd just spent the whole school day with. Messages could be customised with graphics and emojis and you could make the Messenger window on your friend's screen shake to get them to engage with you.

Perhaps in a sign of things to come, another app popular with school kids at the time, BlackBerry Messenger, played a role in coordinating unrest during the riots across several major UK towns and cities in the summer of 2011.[1] These early social networks also first introduced the possibility of what we might now call 'cyberbullying'. MySpace's 'friend ranking' feature, for example, definitely caused a lot of real-life drama and upset among Matteo's friendship groups. In hindsight, these incidents were a glimpse into the dark side of limitless digital communication and its potential for real-world harm.

By the late noughties, everyone (including Matteo's mum) had migrated onto Facebook as the social media platform of choice. Interactivity on Facebook was a lot easier of course, users could easily customise their profile pages, play multiplayer games with friends and embed quizzes and polls for fun. The idea of a person's online 'profile' as an extension of their personality was starting to take hold.

Child development theory holds that adolescence is a vital time for identity-seeking.[2] Gaining the respect and admiration of their peers, even if just from a small friendship group, is crucial to teens' developing self-esteem. This is an entirely normal element of the maturing process where young people will naturally seek greater independence from their adult carers. However, in retrospect, we can see how, even back then, some design features of online platforms could easily exacerbate teenage vulnerabilities.

The widespread adoption of the smartphone and social media has changed the face of how people communicate beyond all recognition within a few years. I think we would all acknowledge that this revolution has come with huge advantages for many of us, including Matteo's mum, still happily exchanging Facebook updates with her Italian siblings. But this societal move to embrace the huge reach of social media and its many useful affordances also marked a shift. The practices of digital communication began to include presenting your online profile to strangers, as well as friends.

Matteo recalls an early awakening to online risk when he accidentally downloaded porn from a 'free' torrent site – the first time he had ever viewed such material – while trying to access episodes of *The A-Team* (which, as some of you may remember, was a corny US action TV series featuring the legendary Mr T). Matteo's parents were pretty unconcerned about what he got up to on the internet, and he certainly would not have dreamed of reporting what he'd seen to them. As far as they knew, he was safely ensconced in his bedroom, far from any danger.

For kids in the late nineties and early noughties, ICT lessons in school focused largely on learning the basics of Microsoft Office. Matteo had had no instruction in online safety, let alone the ethics of how people should conduct themselves online or analyse the content they found there. We wish we could say that this has transformed beyond all recognition, but sadly, owing to the restrictions of the curriculum and a lack of teacher training, digital and media literacy education is still not given the priority it deserves in schools – something for which we've been advocating for ten years at Shout Out UK.

The Roots of the Red Pill

When Matteo looks back on the gender dynamics that were at play in his teenage years, he can acknowledge the prevalence of sexism. Boys at school frequently discussed girls' bodies and he recalls early forms of non-consensual image sharing such as the exchange of nude photos of girls over MSN Messenger. It's important to remember that natural curiosity does play a part in such behaviour. Boys need to be educated about how it is wrong, so they know not to do it, rather than immediately branded as abusers when they do.

What Matteo does not remember from this time was any exposure to the kind of misogynistic narratives which now proliferate in the online media aimed at boys, and which, if we believe the data, may be shaping their attitudes towards women and girls. As a thirty-something herself in the noughties, Amelia can confirm that the divisive discourse focusing on the failings of women and their unfair advantages over men just did not exist in the mainstream as it does today. In fact, as they reached adulthood, many young men of Matteo's generation strove to model their anti-sexist credentials. Relationships between men and women were becoming shaped by women's growing confidence in their own right to live, love and work as they chose.

A small example of how things have changed: when Matteo first started dating, 'going Dutch', where each person paid their share of the night's entertainment, was standard. Now, popular TikTok 'dating coaches' such as Ask Nelly (785,000 followers) push the message that for women to respect them, men must pay the lion's share, not just on a first date, but throughout the relationship.[3]

It felt, to some extent, like models of masculinity were breaking out of the 'man box' we referred to in Chapter Two, to encompass a wider range of qualities and behaviours. This was reflected in popular culture with characters like Tim in the BBC's *The Office*, who rejected the macho culture of David Brent and his sidekicks Gareth and Finchy, to show a more caring and respectful attitude to women.[4] Even Disney made a break from their traditional male leads in 2013's *Frozen*. Kristoff, the true hero of the film (unlike the handsome prince who turns out to be not a nice guy), is honest and supportive and is valued by the heroine, Anna, for his helpful collaboration, rather than his ability to sweep in and 'rescue' her in a dominating fashion.

On the fringes though, the forces of the backlash were steadily gathering.

Back when Matteo was a teen, due to the generally unsupervised nature of his peers' access to the internet at the time, some boys became unhealthily obsessed with websites they'd discovered containing sexual content. These boys tended to be the ones on the fringes of the social scene. For whatever reason – their shyness, nerdiness or inability to fit in – they lacked playground clout and, while not bullied exactly, they were pushed to the margins of peer acceptance. They were the ones who lacked the confidence to talk to girls, often appeared awkward in front of them and struggled to find girlfriends. As they grew older, these were the boys who tended to gravitate towards those figures who offered them a sure-fire way to success with women.

In 2005, investigative journalist Neil Strauss published *The Game: Undercover in the Secret Society of Pickup Artists*, introducing the world to the nascent scene of what became known as pick-up artistry (PUA). He focused mainstream attention on a movement which had been born in early internet chat rooms and forums. Taught by supposedly Casanova-level coaches, the techniques of PUA claimed to be able to turn any man into a success with women. *The Game* was initially intended as a takedown of the movement, but Strauss became sucked into its cult-like ideology. His book, which became a huge bestseller, ended up being followed as a kind of manual by men who felt ignored by women on the dating scene.

The seduction techniques promoted in *The Game* and on the PUA scene, which ultimately became a multimillion-pound industry, were heavy-handed to say the least. They focused on encouraging men to approach as many women in public places as possible with scripted 'lines' calculated to get their phone numbers. Once on a date, men were given a series of steps to follow to get a woman into bed, including escalating to physical contact as quickly as possible and (chillingly) 'Blast Last-Minute Resistance'.[5]

Matteo recalls that, as a boy, he was given no foundational education, either in school PSHE lessons*, or from the wider culture, in the ethics of consent. Without open discussion of these

* PSHE education stands for personal, social, health and economic education, a school curriculum subject in England.

issues, at school, and at home, it is unsurprising that some boys become susceptible to the misogynist belief that overpowering women is acceptable in the pursuit of another notch on the bedpost. This is a point which we will return to later in the book: the modern forces of online misogyny, spread via social networks, are benefiting from pre-existing and persistent educational gaps that still exist, and which we, as parents, urgently need to address.

In his book about the origins of the manosphere, *Lost Boys*, James Bloodworth describes his experiences as a young member of a London cell of Real Social Dynamics, a now notorious commercial company running PUA courses and boot camps. His own story makes clear that, from the beginning, PUA was a narrative that capitalised on young men's insecurities and their perceived inadequacies – any superficial sexual success coming at the expense of authenticity to their own personal qualities and rooted in harmful stereotypes of masculinity and heterosexuality. Here, Bloodworth's coach, Tux, explained the necessity for men to adopt PUA techniques:

> *Tux is a conspiracy theorist. He believes in the existence of a secret society that 52 per cent of the population are part of. Of that 52 per cent, 50 per cent are women and 2 per cent are men. Of that 2 per cent, 1 per cent are gay and the other 1 per cent are sexually attractive 'alpha males' ... According to Tux, everything we have been told about male–female dynamics up to now – by family and friends, by films and soap operas, by popular music – has been a lie ... Propaganda to keep us soft and passive.*[6]

As Bloodworth goes on to explore in his book, we can trace a direct line from this conspiratorial framing of male sexual grievance to the modern-day communities of the manosphere. Even then, this movement was about profiting financially from vulnerable men more than helping them with their problems. Just like PUA, the manosphere is, above all, a commercialised and organised form of misogyny. It leverages men's insecurities about their sexual attractiveness, and sexist myths including that men must be rich to get a girlfriend, to bring vast profits to a few unscrupulous conmen.

The 1970s and 1980s saw the emergence of the men's liberation movement. This was a parallel campaign to women's liberation, looking to challenge stereotypes of masculinity which might be holding men back. Originally supportive of feminism, some elements of this movement switched focus entirely over time to become early proponents of what is now called men's rights activism (MRA). MRA activists claim women's equality harms men. They weaponise the perceived inequalities facing men, particularly in relation to issues like criminal justice, divorce and child custody, to call for an end to feminism and its efforts to address issues like violence against women and women's representation in public life.[7]

It's important to distinguish MRA from those activists, researchers and groups, many of whose work we drew on in Chapter One, who actively work to raise awareness of the real issues facing boys and men. Organisations like the Centre for Policy Research on Men and Boys, Equimundo, Movember, and scholars and writers such as Michael Flood and Debbie Ging work alongside the broader feminist movement, to strategise solutions which push for change to help men and boys. By contrast, the MRA movement, unofficially led by Paul Elam, the US-based founder of the website, blog and forum A Voice For Men, heavily focuses on male grievances and holds women and their 'misandry' (hatred of men) directly responsible for men's unhappiness. Alongside PUA, MRA is the forefather of the modern manosphere and it remains the largest online misogynist community.[8]

In the UK, Justice For Men and Boys (J4MB), is the most well-known native-grown branch of the MRA movement. Founded in 2013 by businessman Mike Buchanan, it was a political party until 2023, running on an explicitly anti-feminist agenda, and fielded candidates in the 2015 general election. Through its political activity, including an association with some figures within the Conservative Party,[9] J4MB has gathered legitimising attention from the mainstream media in the UK, including an interview with Buchanan on ITV's This Morning show.[10]

However, recent research[11] has shown that MRA online activity ranks highly among the various manosphere communities for the use of language justifying violence. Prominent feminists, such as Laura Bates, have been repeatedly targeted by J4MB, through blog content like its 'Whiny Feminist of the Month Award', and attempting to disrupt her public appearances.

Though PUA and MRA both had their early origins in real-world activity, this has continued to migrate online over time, and their advocates remain hugely influential in present day internet communities, despite some seemingly disparate aims and membership. Where they overlap with, and also prefigure, more recent manifestations of online misogyny is in their adherence to the overarching philosophy of the blue and red pill.

The Rabbit Hole

The central 'red pill' terminology of the manosphere is drawn from the 1999 film *The Matrix*, which depicts a dystopian world in which human beings are enslaved by machines, but kept in an unconscious dream-like state.[12] The film's central character Neo is offered the choice of taking a red pill, which will awaken him to reality so he can join the resistance, or a blue pill, which will maintain his state of ignorance and subordination.

The directors of *The Matrix* have spoken out about their concern at the way the narrative of their film has been used in misogynist discourse, since, both openly trans women, they originally intended it as symbolic of their own experience of struggling with gender identity.[13] This core metaphor has been adopted across misogynist groups to represent the idea that our society is dominated by the 'blue pill' illusion that women are not yet treated as equals to men.

Being 'red-pilled' means being woken up to the 'reality' that women, particularly feminists, dominate society, hate men, and are actively working to undermine men's rights.[14] The red pill lore brings together a ragbag assortment of anti-feminist beliefs: in a biological basis for men's 'superiority'; in female 'hypergamy' (in the manosphere, this phrase has been co-opted to mean the '80/20 rule', referred to by Jamie in *Adolescence*, that 80 per cent of women exclusively seek out the top 20 per cent of wealthy and stereotypically 'masculine' men); and in the idea that male violence against women is either a) justified or b) massively overexaggerated.[15] An early locus for men sharing these beliefs was r/TheRedPill, a subreddit which by the mid-2010s had over

140,000 members sharing relatively innocuous advice on how to improve their looks and masturbate less, alongside PUA-inspired dating tips and anti-feminist rants.[16]

Over the past decade or so, the rhetoric of these red-pilled communities has seeped out to spread far and wide across the internet, powering a new age of disturbing misogynist tactics.

Matteo's personal realisation that girls and women might face discrimination and hate solely because of their gender came through gaming. As a teen, he loved historical strategy games like *Crusader Kings* and *Europa Universalis,* which prompted a lifelong love of history. He enjoyed reading posts that gave tips to fellow players in the online communities which grew up around his favourite games, but he also noticed misogynistic attitudes among his gaming peer group. For example, as a young man, Matteo enjoyed a game called *Red Dead Redemption 2,* which was set in America during the era of the Westerns. The game featured historically accurate early women's rights activists (suffragists) as NPCs (non-player characters), and a common 'joke' by some players of the game was to 'lasso' these characters and inflict virtual abuse on them, including tying them to railroad tracks to be run over.[17]

Back then, gaming spaces were even more male-dominated than they are today, and not a lot of thought was given to how actions like these might be fostering narratives harmful to women. In fact, gaming has a long and troubled history of sexism and misogyny. The industry has produced an endless stream of video games portraying female characters as pawns, victims, and objects of male desire. Leaked footage has suggested that, in 2026, Rockstar Games will introduce the very *first* female playable character within the story-driven gameplay of its yet to be released GTA6, with players able to switch between male and female leads.[18] The titans of the industry are only now appearing to put women centre stage.

The industry has also been riddled by allegations of sexual misconduct and harassment. This came to a head in 2014, when online gaming communities became ground zero for heated discussions around sexual discrimination and the role of women within the gaming world.

By this date, gaming had slowly been opening up to more women, both as players and engineers. What became known as Gamergate was an organised backlash against this growing influence: it began with a disgruntled blog post by the ex-boyfriend of games developer Zoë Quinn, falsely claiming that she provided sexual favours to a critic to ensure favourable reviews of one of her games. This allegation was enough to fan the flames of grievance among the substantial misogynist gamer community who inhabited what were still considered fairly fringe corners of the internet, including 4Chan and, of course, Reddit's r/TheRedPill. Claiming that gaming was under attack by the forces of feminism, an online campaign, #gamergate, quickly mobilised, harassing Quinn and other prominent women in the industry.[19] It brought into the mainstream what software engineer Brianna Wu called when Matteo interviewed her in 2022, 'a new playbook for misogyny'.

Following tweets she posted criticising sexism and defending fellow industry professionals, Brianna stirred the Gamergate wrath. She explained:

> *So I got a call one day that 4Chan was starting to investigate me ... This is where they start digging through your entire life to find something to abuse you with. They'll comb through your educational and work history. They'll comb through every tweet you've ever made ... And they will basically bring together a mob to harass you about it. And I could see them organising this mob online. And I realised I had a choice to make. I could stay silent, and I knew it would all blow over in a couple of days ... or I could keep speaking out, and would become a major target.*[20]

Despite being subjected to online abuse, including repeated death and rape threats, Brianna and other women did continue bravely to speak out. But Gamergate proved to be a pivotal moment in the organisation of mass online harassment campaigns against women. It popularised many of the techniques such as doxxing (revealing personal information) and threats of physical violence, which continue to be promoted across the contemporary manosphere and make the internet such a dangerous and unpleasant space for so many women. As one study noted: 'Gamergate was not a passing controversy, but the start of an ongoing culture war that extends far beyond the world of gaming and continues to the present day.'[21]

As we'll see, the spaces associated with gaming remain important recruitment grounds for the forces of misogyny. But Gamergate had also lifted a stone to shed light on the red pill's most feared and notorious cohort: the incels.

The term 'involuntary celibates' ('incels') refers to a group of people who consider themselves unable to attain a sexual partner, though they desire one. It was invented way back in 1997 by a

Canadian woman, known only as 'Alana', who started a supportive site for those struggling to form relationships.[22] In the intervening years, the term has been co-opted by online misogynists. 'Inceldom' has become a well-networked movement with roots on Reddit and 4Chan, gaming lobbies and advice boards, which holds women to blame for men's inability to have a sexual relationship. Like PUAs, incels subscribe to the 80/20 theory of male–female attraction, creating a moral hierarchy in which men are suffering unjustly for women's sexual choosiness in favouring only the richest and most handsome men, the 'alphas'. Unlike PUAs, however, incels see their situation as hopeless; they feel their personal characteristics – whether looks, race or personality – condemn them to a life without sex or romantic love.[23]

Over time, the incel community has formed its own subculture and associated language. Some of this content, including slang and memes, has leaked into mainstream media: for example, 'normies' (socially conformist people) and 'looksmaxxing' (attempting to improve your physical appearance in particular ways). In inceldom, women are classified as 'Staceys' (the most desirable women on the 'sexual marketplace'), and 'Beckys' (average women). Likewise for men, two distinctions are typically made: 'Chads' (the most sexually attractive men), and 'incels' (the rest). The 'Chads' and the 'Staceys' are seen by incel groups as morally and intellectually inferior to the 'Beckys' and the 'incels', but, because they are conventionally good-looking or wealthy, they unfairly claim higher status. The unfortunate 'Beckys' are also derided by incels for ignoring them in favour of trying to snare a 'Chad'.[24] Women deemed unacceptable are frequently dehumanised by incels as 'femoids' or 'foids'.

Like all conspiracy theories, this ideology is rooted in myth and paranoia, which are easy to ridicule. However, among the loose confederacy of the manosphere, it has become the community most closely associated (as in *Adolescence*, for example) with extreme violence.

In 2014, just a few months before the 'gamergate' hashtag went viral, twenty-two-year-old Elliot Rodger uploaded a woman-hating diatribe to YouTube and proceeded to murder six people in Isla Vista, California, injuring fourteen more. Rodger had been a member of an online forum, PUAHate, frequented by men furious that, despite faithful adherence to PUA techniques, they remained unpopular with women.[25] This fuelled a feeling of nihilistic hopelessness within the community, and a sense of rage which was directed at women themselves. Many men on the forum, including Rodger, threatened violence against women, including rape and murder, in revenge.

Alongside several other misogynist murderers, some of whom were explicitly inspired by him, Rodger quickly became a hero and martyr to the nascent incel cause. He has entered its lexicon, with 'going ER' used by incels to mean committing mass murder, and the moniker 'supreme gentleman', by which Rodger referred to himself in a subsequently discovered manifesto, adopted by them as a badge of honour.[26]

Some horrific incidents of extreme violence in the UK over the last few years even led a Home Office review to advise the government in 2025 to extend the definition of terrorism to cover extreme misogyny.[27] In 2021, a twenty-two-year-old man shot and killed five people including his mother in Plymouth, England.[28] The murderer had made posts on YouTube in which he expressed nihilistic views and described incels (a term he identified with) as 'essentially a race of outcasts, abused and forgotten by humanity' who deserve 'a better place in society'. He went on: 'I personally don't think once you live this life you can really ever change ... The damage done, even if you become "millionaire Chad" tomorrow, I personally believe my scars and damage will follow me forever and I'm sure others feel the same.'[29] Another man, arrested in 2019 in Middlesbrough for planning a terrorist attack had visited incel websites and appeared to admire Elliot Rodger. The star and co-creator of *Adolescence*, Stephen Graham, has also confirmed that the show was inspired by his shock at a similar incident where a young boy stabbed a girl.[30]

Incel-related violence has captured a lot of attention and outrage, but leading expert Meadhbh Park, author of *Blackpilled*, a book based on her own interviews with incels, feels that this has overshadowed something just as integral to the incel philosophy as violence against women: a commitment to nihilism and the desire for self-annihilation. Some in the incel community still hold on to the idea that they will one day 'ascend' (lose their virginity and join 'normie' society), by striving to fit the masculine ideal they believe women prefer. To this end they often embark on extreme exercise programmes, taking steroids and other forms of 'looksmaxxing'. Many more have completely given up on the idea that society or women will ever value them, and have taken the 'black pill', succumbing to total despair and the belief they may as well 'LDAR' (lie down and rot).

Matteo interviewed Meadhbh for another of our Shout Out UK *Media Minded* podcasts and, according to her, the incel movement actually holds as much of a threat to its own members as anybody else. She described spending time in incel forums where young men frequently discuss killing themselves, where they are encouraged to do so by others and where those who have committed suicide are praised and idealised.[31]

What makes this particularly disturbing is that incels make up the youngest cohort of the manosphere, with the vast majority in their teens to mid-twenties.[32] Some boys, who should be taking their first steps into the world of dating and relationships, hanging out and chatting with women and girls in seminars and school grounds, are instead falling for the idea that their situation is so desperate they should resort to suicide. It is a horrifyingly sad state of affairs.

Another massively influential subcommunity among the younger men of the red pill ecosystem is made up of those who believe men can only be happy if they reject any contact with women whatsoever. 'Men going their own way' (MGTOW) is a huge and growing movement of online forums, vloggers and influencers who share the world view that society is biased against men.[33] They repeat many of the tropes which have been central to the older MRA philosophy, such as that women exploit men by using relationships and marriage to extract their wealth and emotional support, taking these even further.[34] Central to MGTOW philosophy is the idea that the incidence of sexual violence by men against women is massively overestimated and that the vast majority of rape claims are false and used by women to control and punish men.

As we have seen elsewhere in the manosphere, MGTOW fans also rely heavily on widely debunked theories from evolutionary psychology, for example, that women are biologically programmed to act in their own best interests, which run counter to men's. A popular community hashtag is #AWALT or 'all women are like that'. Ironically, men subscribing to MGTOW are often among those who mobilise behind the #NotAllMen hashtag used online to denounce those working to end male violence against women.

What has given the movement particular force in recent years is that its distinctive blend of paranoia and virulent hatred has been massively amplified to young men across vlogging sites such as YouTube.[35] Its preferred narrative of traditional masculinity under attack by evil feminists has also been echoed and seized upon by elements of the far right, and even mainstream figures such as YouTube psychologist Jordan Peterson and media personality Piers Morgan, who uses clickbait attacks on feminism (a typical example, according to Morgan, being James Bond actor Daniel Craig carrying his baby in a papoose), to stoke the rage of his online following.[36]

As we've indicated earlier in the chapter, what unites the misogynists of the red pill is *not* fighting the cause for men and boys in order to improve their lives. In *Lost Boys*, James Bloodworth quotes a former MGTOW follower remarking on the central contradiction of MGTOW: 'They said they were *men going their own way*; yet all they did was complain about women.'[37]

One of the central aims of all these communities is to roll back gender equality by promoting misogynistic lies which make the world more dangerous for women and girls and actually also diminish men's emotional lives and their mental and physical health.[38] Despite the labyrinthine complexity of the movement with its subgroups, sects and internal arguments and schisms, it really is as simple as that.

Its other, equally important objective? Money.

Enter the Algorithm

If you are a male internet user under sixty who has searched online for fitness content, dating advice, or nutrition guides; if you've been in a gaming lobby or related Discord server, or read the YouTube comments on a video about a male celebrity who has been accused of sexual harassment, we can pretty much guarantee that you've been in an online space where recruitment for extreme misogyny is taking place.

In the early days of the movement we've described, men and boys had to actively seek out hateful content in forums and Reddit threads. That is no longer the case. Social media and video-sharing sites have brought the margins to the mainstream, transforming and speeding up the pathway to online radicalisation. These days, extreme content is likely to find you, whether you look for it or not. Depending on your age, predisposition and environment, you may not even recognise it as extreme.

Over the past fifteen years, the tech companies behind the social media apps we use every day have pivoted to a mantra of 'personalisation' that prioritises user retention. Since their business model rests on selling advertising to users, platforms are engineered to maximise the time spent on-site. To this end, they build in addictive software features such as 'likes', scrolling and swiping, which give us all mini dopamine hits to keep us hooked, and notifications which pop up to make sure we check our phones every five minutes.

They also use algorithmic optimisation to predict what users would like to see in their feeds, and give them more, similar content. If I, for example, a fictional teenage boy, watch one TikTok video on how to build muscle through bodybuilding to the end, the algorithm will clock that I am interested in it. Since TikTok's ad revenue is dependent on my engagement, I am highly likely to receive more, similar videos. And, since content which elicits strong emotions receives higher engagement from users (comments, likes, etc.), these are in turn, more likely to surface in my feed.[39]

In our counter-extremism work at Shout Out UK, we call this the 'echo chamber effect'. These algorithms can work so effectively that a user's particular world view (which the algorithm determines through their level of engagement with each piece of content) is reinforced and rarely challenged by opposing perspectives.[40] Many experts and commentators now believe that this is one reason for the rising political polarisation we see across the world – including an increase in misogynistic attitudes. The content served to boys and young men relating to women, masculinity and gender is often highly divisive and provocative, leading to what might be termed 'algorithmic gender polarisation'.

So, if a boy, rejected by a girl at school and feeling entirely normal (but usually fleeting) feelings of resentment and insecurity, sees a post about women which validates his feelings of victimisation and drops a 'like', the algorithm notes this and will serve up more of the same content, which can quickly become more extreme over time. His algorithm will also surface the most popular content engaged with by users whose demographic characteristics, such as age and gender, match his own.

Exactly how these predictive algorithms work varies across tech platforms and is often not transparent, but repeated research and experiments have shown the echo chamber, sometimes also known as the 'filter bubble', to be a very real phenomenon. A recent report by Commonsense Media found that, when it came to teenage boys who had viewed masculinity content online, 68 per cent said that it just appeared in their feed without them searching for it. Much of the content that they were encountering contained sexist messaging, with 48 per cent seeing content on TikTok that suggested girls only want to date certain kinds of men and around a fifth encountering messages on TikTok and Instagram that boys are treated unfairly compared to girls. The same study also found that boys who had encountered the most problematic masculinity content were those with fewer real-world connections and lower self-esteem.[41]

If big tech's algorithms are generating profit from boys who are feeling lonely or isolated and lacking in confidence, the same can also be said for those who produce this polarising content. As we've outlined, sexual success with women and the ability to make money are two essential pillars of being a man in the 'man box' of the patriarchy. Adolescent boys are highly likely to be curious about online messaging which promises them an easy route to either of these, and their engagement with such content online can generate riches for its creators.

The framework of the manosphere which we've described has grown into a huge network of massively popular YouTubers, streamers and podcasters reaping personal fortunes from the online platforms' ad revenue-sharing models. They have also profited from the wider fame they've gained as a result of this algorithmic virality, to spin a huge ecosystem of online 'training' and subscriptions. Andrew Tate, the most notorious of these, has, as documented by journalists Jamie Tahsin and Matt Shea, leveraged his online following to build a business empire of motivational courses, in-person boot camps and the alleged sexual exploitation of women.[42]

At the height of his fame in 2022, Tate boasted more than 4.7 million followers on Instagram and 5 million on TikTok, where his videos were viewed an estimated 12 billion times.[43] He has since been widely 'deplatformed' on social media as a result of repeated misogynistic, racist and homophobic comments.[44] Tate's popularity has waned further following criminal charges of rape and human trafficking brought against him in the UK and Romania. He remains, however, active on X, having been reinstated to the platform when it was bought by Elon Musk in 2022, and 'fan' accounts on TikTok and YouTube continue to spread his videos.[45] His many business ventures prey on young men who may be susceptible to the view that riches and the domination of women should be men's primary aspirations.

Those, for example, who believe the '41 Tenets' for masculine success promoted on Tate's website, which include: 'I seek to help men overcome poor mental health through embracing hard work, physical improvements and shared masculine brotherhood' can pay him $8,000 to join the War Room, according to the site, 'a global network in which exemplars of individualism work to free the modern man from socially induced incarceration'. Tahsin and Shea's investigation into the War Room found its students were, in fact, being tutored by Tate in how to violently groom women into carrying out sex work.[46]

Tate's influence may be somewhat neutered, but a raft of copycat hyper-macho 'manfluencers' are still actively flooding boys' social media feeds. Misogynist messages are often embedded in content that chimes with boys' legitimate interests and fears. Influencers such as Adin Ross and Sneako started out posting gaming advice; the hosts of *Fresh and Fit*, the hugely popular US-based manosphere podcast, advertise themselves as experts in dating and fitness. Hamza Ahmed, one of the most popular British masculinity influencers, peddles highly sexist and women-blaming narratives under the guise of 'personal development' videos.[47] And yes, you can also sign up for his online course, Library of Adonis, starting from $37 a month.

Even where misogynist content creators have been deplatformed, most of them are easily able to move to less regulated sites and apps where their content can still be surfaced. We've seen evidence that vulnerable young men are being led from more open online spaces such as public gaming lobbies or YouTube comments sections, to closed channels such as Discord servers or Telegram chat rooms where more extreme content can be shared.[48] Thankfully, only a small proportion of boys will go all the way down the rabbit hole to violent misogynist extremism. But many, many more are absorbing a daily drip feed of hateful content, cynically aimed at monetising their everyday adolescent challenges.

In Chapter Six, we will take a deeper dive into the world boys inhabit online, and the effect it has on their lives. But now, let's hear from some boys themselves, in their own words.

PART TWO
SYMPTOMS

Chapter 4
Boys Unfiltered

In our work at Shout Out UK, we like to emphasise listening to young people and devising solutions *with* them, rather than *about* them. So, in addition to the data we've drawn on so far about life today for British boys and young men, we decided to conduct some interviews to give us a snapshot of the thoughts and feelings of young men in their own words. The interviews took place online so participants from several UK regions could join and we made sure all the young people were paid to mitigate against socio-economic bias. To keep the sample as broadly representative as possible, we recruited participants via our UK-wide organisational networks and through targeted, paid social media ads.

We focused on boys who are in their last years of school, or have recently left, as this is the cohort that grew up in the era of Andrew Tate and the developing influence of the manosphere, as examined up to this point in the book. How was it influencing their feelings about girls, women, dating and their futures? Let's ask Zain (eighteen), Adam (eighteen), Martin (seventeen) and Faisal (eighteen), who are all sixth-form students, and Adrian (twenty), who is at university. We've disguised their identities with pseudonyms, but the quotes are all in their own words – with some edits for clarity.

> *'I do think phones are actually a good thing, in many ways.'* – ***Adam, eighteen***

We began by asking the boys and men about their internet use and the amount of time they generally spend online every day. Seventeen-year-old Martin's response was fairly typical: 'My screen time averages around five hours on my phone per day, with an hour and a half of that being me messaging people on Snapchat and around two hours on other social media.' When asked how long he spent on his phone per scrolling session, Faisal (eighteen) likewise estimated, 'At least two or three hours. I think the most I've ever done is like five, but I try to keep it within that two-to-three-hour range.'

The boys all mentioned YouTube, Instagram, Snapchat and TikTok as their platforms of choice, with a couple also already on LinkedIn as preparation for future employment opportunities. Adrian was also a keen Redditor and Martin was a user of X.

Some of the boys and men expressed anxiety about the amount of time they were spending on social media, with TikTok emerging as the platform they found the most addictive. Adrian, the oldest interviewee at twenty, commented, 'TikTok's definitely the most addictive, no doubt. You can spend literally just six hours sitting watching TikTok. Obviously, I'm not saying I do, but that's kind of what it's designed for.' He continued, 'It has done really bad things for my attention span, to be honest. I feel like it's become a lot harder to watch films and do work. I know it sounds bad but I always see this as a very common sentiment on social media.'

Adam (eighteen) shared a compulsion to check social media frequently: 'You just have the urge to pick up the phone and scroll. Not even out of enjoyment. It's just the urge.' When asked if he considered himself addicted to his phone, Adam replied, 'I'm 100 per cent addicted. Yeah, of course. I would say everyone in my generation is.'

I think a lot of us, parents as well as young people, can relate to this worry: the addictive nature of most social media platforms is pretty much a given in modern society – and backed by data, of course.[1]

As our conversation turned to a possible social media ban for under-sixteens, Adam professed himself, like many young people, vigorously opposed to the idea. Making the case for teen mobile phone use, he said, 'Maybe this is an unpopular opinion, but I do think phones are actually a good thing in many ways. I feel like I also educate myself using my phone to read things. I'm not just looking at brain rot 24/7. So even though I do think it's definitely been bad for my [school] work, I also think it's been good for my knowledge, if that makes sense, to have a repertoire of infinite knowledge and information.' Asked to define 'brain rot', he clarified, 'It's just sort of meaningless. It's like the end result of Gen Z humour, I guess, which is very absurd and ironic.'

Faisal and Adam were both regular users of Instagram and found it as compelling as TikTok. Faisal remarked, 'You can't stop scrolling different reels and stuff like that. I'm a very big sports fan, so I'll see a lot of sports-related content, but there are times where the algorithm shows these reels, some of which convey opinions that I agree with and some convey opinions which I don't agree with.'

When asked to clarify the kind of opinions that he was referring to, it became clear that Faisal meant politically polarising content, including misogynistic viewpoints. He went on, 'I would see this sort of content mainly on Instagram because, in my personal opinion, Instagram has looser rules in terms of what can be seen, what can't be seen and what can be produced. I feel like TikTok's much stricter. TikTok's more of a kids' app compared to Instagram.'

Adam was scathing of the idea that TikTok was a safer environment for kids, however: 'TikTok is the place that fake news thrives in, really. And it's the place for dumb people to express opinions that they probably shouldn't be expressing.'

When asked where he came across the most divisive or hateful content, Zain (eighteen) agreed, 'So I'll say TikTok is number one'; but he quickly added, 'Then it's Snapchat, because Snapchat is a very discreet messaging app. You can easily talk to people and, especially in my generation, Snapchat is where you can commit digital crime – sending unwanted images or stuff like that.'

Zain didn't wish to elaborate on whether he was aware of his peers being engaged in activity like this, but, when pressed, he expanded, 'Snapchat is known as a dangerous platform to be using and can easily get you into trouble with the public law.' This comment suggests an awareness of the legal consequences of image-based abuse – possibly learned via school PSHE lessons, where the programme of study has recently been updated to cover this issue.

Martin's social media consumption was mainly on X and Instagram. He explained, 'I use X, mainly, as it is the best place to have debates and find news regarding football, but I have witnessed situations in which people have received hate for comments or views they have left online. X, in particular, is becoming quite polarised and political. I see political content dominating my feed despite the fact I don't engage with it. I also think that Instagram Reels is not a great space, with there being lots of graphic and racist media being posted and not taken down.'

Despite its notoriety as a cradle of inceldom, Adrian made the case for Reddit as a platform where users were actually exposed to a wider range of views than on most: 'You know, the popular perception of Reddit is completely false. Reddit's very progressive, very intellectual compared to TikTok.'

None of the boys posted very actively on social media, and in most cases, their activity was limited to scrolling their feeds for entertainment. At the start of his interview, Adam confessed, 'I feel like I have quite boring social media usage, I don't comment on stuff. I barely "like" things. I only "like" things that I want to watch again because obviously you can go back to it. So I'm never commenting, "Oh, I enjoyed that!"' He also stated, rather dismissively, 'A lot of the time people just have very poor opinions and shout a lot of nonsense on the internet.'

Ofcom's extensive media reports on children's online habits confirm that this is a nationwide phenomenon: with each passing year, young people are becoming more and more reluctant to create posts on social media, perhaps wary of the pitfalls of peer disapproval or ridicule. This is despite some evidence that shows that the mental health of young people who actively create their own content is better than those who just passively consume others'.[2]

'They just want to make money off you, basically.'
– Zain, eighteen

The young men all showed an awareness that social media algorithms often served them content that they were not necessarily seeking out, and they proceeded to tell us how engaging with posts on such mainstream topics as fitness and self-development could quickly cause their feed to be flooded with more divisive messaging.

Adam noted how being rich is framed as an essential element of being a man in much of the content he sees online: 'There's a lot of masculinity stuff online, especially in regards to making money. There's a lot of posts about how you need to start your own businesses and be loaded by the time you're like twenty-one. There's a lot of crypto stuff directed at young men. All the crypto stuff seems very tied to masculinity.' He continued, 'I mean maybe people think that young men want to be loaded, but I think a lot of it is tied to being more manly because, whenever you see it, it is always tied to these sort of fitness posts and the eating raw steak nonsense.'

Martin was also aware that self-help content sometimes crossed a line: 'I do quite like motivational influencers, but I think in terms of misogynistic content this is where things can become unintentionally dangerous. There are some brilliant creators – David Goggins, Matthew McConaughey, etc. But many who begin in this vein can turn. A great example is Andrew Tate, who initially was promoting ways for young men to improve their lives and then revealed more offensive views.'

Although some of the boys did not recognise the term manosphere, they were all aware of how content using some of its ideas can be monetised by online creators. Zain classed this as 'scam' activity, observing, 'I've seen on social media people who try to say, "Buy my course, you can make more money" and all this stuff. There's people who show lavish lifestyles, saying "buy my course or text me or message me" and then they'll sell you a course. They're all basically scams. They just want to make money off you.' Zain also noted that if every boy took one of the enormous number of 'how to be an influencer' courses offered by these figures, then the market for influencers would quickly become over-saturated: 'At the end of the day, if you go into their market, then they're going to end up losing money!'

Faisal, who enjoys fitness content on Instagram, reported having seen posts and ads promoting 'masculinity' and finance courses, as well as those selling quack supplements claiming to boost testosterone. However, he felt unmoved by them: 'I've always taken no notice of it. I get that it's there and I get that people are promoting it, but I've never really thought, "Oh, I need to do that," but I can see that a lot of people might. I just don't think I care really. I just think it's daft and I find it more amusing than factual.'

Of all the interviewees, Adrian was the one who had seen most looksmaxxing content, and was following the online journey of Clavicular, a Kick streamer notorious for promoting cosmetic procedures: 'I've never done it myself, but I do see lots of posts of people showing how they've gone from looking very bad to looking attractive using looksmaxxing, and how it's improved their success in dating. I didn't necessarily see it as a bad thing.' Adrian appeared to admire how Clavicular had turned himself from 'mid'-looking into a 'Chad' (in his words).

'I feel like misogynistic is a loaded term.'
– Adrian, twenty

Over the course of our conversations with boys around perceptions of masculinity, feminism and the manosphere, they did express some takes which we'd classify as outright misinformation, but these were far outnumbered by those expressing simple confusion, as well as some nuanced and perceptive reflections. The overall picture was one of young men desperately trying to get to grips with the conflicting messages that were being presented to them about masculinity, relationships and their place in the world as men.

Adrian defined masculinity as 'the social expectations regarding how men should behave, such as how they should be strong, providers, dominant'.

When asked to describe what makes a man, Faisal gave quite an idealistic view: 'I feel like a true man is someone who serves their community. I don't really know how to explain this ... someone who is moral, someone who cares for others, someone who won't back down when they're being challenged. I feel like that's how I perceive a man.'

Zain's epitome of a man represented strength and commanded respect – 'someone who does not take bullying and is able to get people to respect them' – but went further, implying dominance: 'Also if they do get in a relationship [with a woman] then they have to be superior, or in my opinion I don't think it will work.' He also referred to a need to 'feel you are respected by other boys. It's about the other boys being scared of you and not saying bad things about you.'

Masculinity as something that is policed by other boys and men is a theme we will return to later in the book. But it's clear from Zain's comments here that being regarded negatively, not 'tough' or 'masculine', not 'man enough', by their male peers, is something to be feared.

The boys and men had a limited understanding of the concept of 'patriarchy'. Zain mistook it for 'patriotism', venturing: 'The term patriarchy is in my opinion about protecting your own country from war and invasion and, from the right-wing perspective, immigrants.'

Faisal offered the following reflection: 'I perceive patriarchy as a negative term. I don't know how to put it, but it is a very looked down upon term, like something that needs to be demolished, that needs to be torn down.' He also expressed an awareness that the idea of 'toxic masculinity' might be influencing how men are regarded by women (as potential dating partners) which made him feel defensive: 'Men are all perceived [by girls] as criminals and just very horrible people. And I feel like that can distance men away from having a partner, a sensual partner. They're not perceived in the right way from their partner's perspective. So that's my viewpoint. I won't say I've put a barrier up, but I am much more careful of how people perceive me and how I present myself.'

When it came to the online manosphere, Zain was clear: 'I've never heard that term before ever in my life.' Faisal, however, had a good grasp, saying: 'I always perceive it to be something like an ideology that's wanting male domination. Exterminating feminism, stuff like that.' Martin was a little unsure, but his reply was in the right ballpark: 'I believe it refers to the movement which opposes feminism and also believes that men deserve different or more favourable treatment in society.'

Adrian also understood the concept of the manosphere, but pushed back on the suggestion that all content associated with it was inherently misogynistic: 'I feel like misogynistic is a loaded term. What's very common and what seems to be the dominant view among men [online] is more traditional views on women, if that makes sense, that women shouldn't really be going out clubbing and, you know, sleeping with random people, that women should be listening to men, should be more submissive. I guess that would be more common than, you know, "I hate women".'

> *'I do think there's a lot of young lads being funny, playing devil's advocate just to get a reaction out of people.'* – **Adam, eighteen**

One phenomenon that all the boys and men *had* heard of was the ubiquitous Andrew Tate. However, their views on him were largely negative. At least according to our sample, the shock value that brought Tate playground notoriety a few years ago appears to be waning. Faisal, possibly echoing what he had heard from an older adult, said of Tate: 'He has been accused of, you know, human trafficking and rape. So he is a very bad person.'

Adam, although he observed, 'Andrew Tate's not really around much any more,' told us that when he was a younger boy at school, Tate's content was much discussed in his friendship groups. 'I wouldn't say any of the boys in my group hated Andrew Tate. None of us liked him either. We just sort of took the piss out of what he was saying. There's a few lads who I remember at my school taking what he said on board and being a bit like, "Oh, I need to act more manly and do this kind of stuff." It was never the lads who were in a big social group who were affected. I'd say the lads who were more isolated, or on the edge of the friendship group, seemed to take it on board a lot more, which I always found weird.'

Adam went on to describe how most boys in his friend group at school had actually distanced themselves from one self-professed Tate fan. He explained: 'The girls had a big opinion about him, and then everyone was just like, "What do we do, because we don't really want to be affiliated with someone who is saying things like that?" If his name came up, the girls would be like, "Oh, he follows Andrew Tate blah blah blah."' He finished: 'Eventually, I think he just got more isolated and then became friends with other people, because no one I know really speaks to him any more or has any connection with him.'

It's interesting to note that, in this case, a boy's expression of Tate fandom led to him being frozen out by peers. We can only hope that this ostracism didn't backfire and lead to him to connect with 'other people' who took him further down the misogyny rabbit hole.

Adrian felt that Tate's influence among schoolboys, even at the height of his fame, had been overstated by the media, since he didn't actually recall viewing much of his content himself: 'I feel like before Elon Musk took over X it was very difficult to even see this content [misogynistic influencers], for me at least. I feel like everything was very heavily censored. [Tate] was almost a myth in many ways. His videos would be deleted, you know, days after they were posted on YouTube. And there was just this massive censorship drive that really just made him more popular.' When asked what he made of Tate himself, Adrian confessed, 'I thought he was funny, as in, he reminded me of a Sacha Baron Cohen character, and I think he is just quite a funny person in general. But I always found him very dodgy, you know.'

Adam agreed that Tate 'does seem like a character cos what he says is just so overexaggerated', and he also expressed doubt that boys actually believed in his ideology. He felt that, most of the time, boys repeated his views as 'banter' among peers, aimed at either impressing other boys or shocking girls: 'I think a lot of the time it's all bravado. A lot of the time they're just mocking it and joking about it. And I think that can get lost a lot of the time, and then that leads to a lot of negative views coming up about young men. But obviously, yeah, there's a lot of people saying things for effect. I do think there's a lot of young lads being funny, playing devil's advocate just to get a reaction out of people.'

Zain was critical of Andrew Tate, regarding him as one of the 'scammers' he'd alluded to earlier in our interview: 'Andrew Tate's an attention seeker in my opinion cos he purely wants to make money. The more views he can get [of his videos online], the more people who are talking about him, the more will probably sign up to one of his courses. Someone like, I think it's James Morgan or something [Piers Morgan], he interviews people and then he starts arguing with them. People like him also want to make money by interviewing someone like Andrew Tate.'

Despite Andrew Tate's content being harder to find these days on social media, Zain is spot on when he suggests that some media figures, like Piers Morgan, do indeed continue to give him and other hate-filled influencers a platform, no doubt in order to bolster their own viewing figures.[3] Adrian also noted how following Elon

Musk's acquisition of X in 2022, his social feed turned darker: 'On Twitter, it was quite crazy. All these influencers, who have been banned everywhere, they show up on Twitter and are just absolutely massive, you know, getting hundreds of thousands of likes.'

Despite the boys' ambivalence towards Andrew Tate, we wanted to gauge how much they had seen and absorbed of the sexist ideology he has come to represent. Our conversations turned towards dating, and relations between the sexes.

> *'I feel like being able to communicate with each other is a very key skill.'* – ***Faisal, eighteen***

Some of the boys expressed the view that women, while they professed to want equality with men and to be treated with respect, actually preferred men who were stereotypically macho and aggressive – which Zain referred to as the 'drug dealer type'. Zain's evidence for this was a popular YouTube/TikTok trope where streamers ask women on the street which they'd rather date: 'nice guy' or 'drug dealer'. He explained: 'Most females in my generation are playing a part in how a man should be, before being in a relationship with them, I feel. It does have a conflict with the idea of feminism, or how a woman should be respectfully treated. There's ideas of most women wanting a man to basically look like a drug dealer. I saw the clips on TikTok. I think there was a clip from the YouTubers called the Sidemen.'[4]

When we asked him to tell us more about the kind of men women wanted to date, he elaborated: 'They essentially have to have no manners, basically act like everyone has to be scared of them and everyone has to give them respect.'

It has long been a cliché that women prefer 'bad boys' to 'nice guys' and this stereotype appears to have persisted and become even stronger among Gen Z. Zain finds women's attitudes 'very contradictory ... they will be like, "Oh, he's a bad person" and all that stuff. But at the end of the day, Andrew Tate says stuff they would expect the "drug dealer" partner to be saying. So what he's saying about how to treat a female, basically I feel like that's what you're going to have to do if you want to be in a relationship.'

Adrian also had a rather pessimistic view of women, which seemed influenced by negative stereotypes he'd seen online. When we challenged him on this, he responded that rather than being misogynistic, his views were realistic: 'It's more about the perceived issues with the women of this generation. I guess the main perception is they're quite demanding of men. People often say that women will be feminists on every issue except dating. They expect a lot from men and aren't really willing to give a whole lot back, is kind of the main perception.'

We asked if this observation was borne out by his real-life experiences, to which he replied: 'I see a lot of TikToks of women talking about being promiscuous or talking about how to manipulate men. And you'd see a lot of men in the comments being like, "Oh, these women are our future wives."'

In both cases, the boys appeared to extrapolate from attitudes they'd seen in viral content online, assuming they also applied to the real world. We didn't sense much in the way of reflection from them about how these posts might have become viral in the first place precisely because they contained emotional 'rage bait' calculated to annoy them. Despite our prompting, neither boy gave examples of girls they knew in real life who behaved like those in the TikTok videos they cited.

We asked Adam if he too had noticed divisive content pitting young women against young men. He was a little more reflective, replying: 'I think there is a lot of that online – comparing the behaviours between boys and girls. But when I see it, it always feels like these things are so overexaggerated and the people putting it out there are so ridiculous that I always take no notice of it. But there's a lot of it out there – like what men do in relationships as opposed to what women do and stereotypes of what they should and shouldn't do.'

Martin had seen misogynist posts on social media: 'Yes, in terms of content such as the likes of Andrew Tate and in the form of hate comments and replies. These are most prevalent on X and Instagram reels, which I feel do not take as much action in removing harmful content.' He condemned it, noting the presence of hateful comments directed at women even in the comments section of fairly innocuous posts: 'It upsets me to see people treated in such a way, especially for something which they cannot control. I am often shocked, not only by how someone can hold those views but also the huge amount of positive engagement these posts receive from other people.'

On a more positive note, when we asked whether he thought this online environment reflected growing division between the sexes, Faisal said he thought most young people still wanted a loving, secure relationship above all else: 'In my personal experience, I'd say it's more to do with protecting one another, making sure both are safe within their own environment. I feel like being able to communicate with each other is a very key skill.'

'Both boys and girls face their own challenges.'
– Faisal, eighteen

We were keen to learn if the boys and young men subscribed to the belief that feminism has gone too far to the extent that young men are actively being discriminated against.

Faisal thought it possibly had: 'I agree with the main message [of feminism], women deserve equality and stuff like that, but it's very difficult to sort of pinpoint exactly when it went too far. There is this overgeneralisation of male behaviour. Some feminist rhetoric has been criticised for painting all men as horrible sexists and oppressors, which can alienate men against feminists. So, for instance, I remember a few years ago there was a social media campaign with the hashtag #menaretrash. That's an example of overgeneralising male behaviour to a point where males don't want to associate with feminist rhetoric.'

Adrian felt there was definitely hostility from boys in his school to the idea of feminism: 'I remember in school, a lot of my friends would always be very anti-feminist. Like their view of feminists is people who don't like men, basically.'

Zain associated feminism with 'attacking religions like Islam because a woman has to wear certain pieces of clothing ... just attacking, rather than understanding and learning about it and why that's there'.

Adam had gathered a nuanced perspective on gender discrimination from studying English Language at A level. He explained: 'We did a lot on gender stereotypes and all that. They always talked about how gender is built around stereotypes being repeated, as opposed to an actual, like, physical thing. I remember we talked a lot about gaming and the use of Xbox and how it's not massive in women as opposed to men, and so there's a lot of bad language and stuff used around men as opposed to women.'

When asked if boys or girls have it easier, Zain felt girls had some advantages: 'I would say both have it difficult, but I would say it's probably easier for girls. In the workplace I feel like it's easier for girls to get a promotion especially if the manager is a male, because if that girl builds a relationship with that manager, then the manager will likely give that girl a promotion.'

Again, we wondered where Zain had gathered this assumption and he replied: 'I saw on TikTok how someone got fired from McDonald's for basically rejecting the manager from getting closer. So he wanted to get closer, like, get into a relationship with the female, and then she decided not to and got fired ... Imagine if that female did accept it then possibly she would get a promotion which would give the ability to earn more in that workplace.' We can't be sure which TikTok video Zain is referring to here, but McDonald's workplace culture has been in the spotlight over the last couple of years for not doing enough to protect staff from sexual harassment.[5] Zain's framing of a manager who wanted to 'get closer' as a promotion opportunity which a young woman would be foolish to turn down seems to indicate a confused notion of consent.

He did then go on to concede, 'If the woman doesn't want it, then they feel uncomfortable at the workplace and they'll keep feeling uncomfortable and not wanting to be there and it can affect their mental health. Also, it's dangerous for the male, of course, because if they do get caught, then they will get punished and then they might start having regrets.'

A popular theme in the manosphere is that women are curtailing men's opportunities in the workplace, and this argument is one which may resonate with young men who are struggling economically. Some of the boys we spoke to did express money worries when we asked about the issues that were most important to them. Martin said: 'My biggest worry is student debt, probably for me financially, I would love to attend uni but with the interest rates I struggle to see myself paying off the loan and am likely to repay it twice over before the debt is wiped.'

On the question of whether boys had it harder in the current economic climate, Faisal said: 'I feel like both boys and girls face their own challenges. So I would try not to see it through a gender landscape. I see it more through class and not having opportunities available for both boys and girls. That's how I would see it.' He went on to acknowledge that the sexual double standard did tend to work in boys' favour, with girls penalised more heavily by peers for their dress, sexual behaviour, dating record, etc.: 'If girls screw up, they get blamed much more than a boy would. The girl is held much more responsible.'

An area where the boys also felt they were worse off than girls was in terms of feeling potentially threatened with physical violence. Faisal maintained that 'boys suffer much more bullying', and for Zain 'being respected, ensuring no other boy is bullying you' was a very real concern. Though not necessarily based on his own experience, he expressed the worry that arguments fuelled by online toxicity among boys his age might spill over into real-world violence: 'Young people can take arguments that happen online to in person, stabbing each other and the consequences that come from that.'

> *'My parents questioned me on my views on Tate, but no one ever told me about the dangers of online echo chambers or how to spot harmful content in general.'* – **Martin, seventeen**

We were keen to learn from the boys how they felt about adults' involvement in their digital lives – were they aware of the difficulties reported by the boys in navigating this sometimes divisive environment?

Adam's parents had restricted his access to social media as a younger boy. He told us: 'We weren't allowed social media till we were going into secondary school, maybe year eight. So, it was always just messaging friends, which was harmless, obviously.' He then went on to explain that while social media platforms were out of bounds, his parents allowed him access to YouTube, where he watched gaming videos, among others: 'I watched a lot of GTA [Grand Theft Auto] videos and stuff when I was like ten, so it's probably not great cos it's a very violent graphic game.'

While his parents were likely unaware that Adam was watching videos like this, he did feel that they had done their best to protect him: 'They tried to stop me watching bad stuff, but it's very easy to click on the wrong thing, watch the wrong thing. You know, online there's a lot of horrible stuff. Well, it's harder now because on YouTube you have to have ID to prove that you're over eighteen or over sixteen, but especially when I was like ten to twelve, you could just watch anything.'[6]

Zain, though he wished he could, felt unable to discuss the things he saw on social media with his parents. His reasons were complex: 'They're from a different generation ... they don't understand what social media is and what it's for. And also, speaking English as a second language is very difficult for them – they're not used to what social media basically is, or misogyny or how this generation is. They just turn a blind eye. They're just getting on with daily life, basically, and trying to give advice on how to live life, like, for example, go to university, go to education, and all of that traditional stuff.'

And Faisal echoed this: 'It's very difficult to speak with my parents who are from a different generation. They don't understand the difficulties that are faced in modern society, and they don't understand how social media works and the things we see there. So, it's very difficult to have that conversation.' When asked if he would ever tell them if he'd seen something online that worried or confused him, he continued, 'Obviously I do see stuff like that, but I try to like deal with that stuff on my own accord because since I am a young man, I'm much more likely to resolve it in a more simple way, rather than get my parents involved.'

Adrian didn't have much confidence that his parents could help him either, and reported: 'My parents would just say, "Ignore it" or tell me to get off social media permanently.'

Martin felt strongly that the adults in his life were not addressing online misogyny in an effective way: 'My parents questioned me on my views on Tate, but no one ever told me about the dangers of online echo chambers or how to spot harmful content in general.' We asked if the issue had been discussed at school, to which he replied, 'It is addressed somewhat at school, but it is slightly superficial and I feel as though they don't truly understand the issue. A lot of the focus will be placed on treating girls and women with respect, for example, rather than addressing underlying beliefs and why they are wrong. I also feel like a lot of time was invested into Andrew Tate, when he was just a singular creator spreading harmful messages – instead, more education could've been placed on misogyny online as a whole.'

Martin's thoughtful remark is striking. We share his belief that we can only tackle online misogyny by educating both kids and ourselves about these 'underlying beliefs'. And this does start in the home. If they could wave a magic wand to make parents more knowledgeable about the realities of their kids' online lives, we asked, would they do it? All the boys replied, 'Yes.'

As we looked back on the interview transcripts, we agreed that, initially, some of the boys' responses possibly followed what they thought we might want to hear as the authors of a book on anti-misogyny. But, as the conversation progressed, their reflections became much more unfiltered and honest. We were struck again and again by their honesty and self-reflection. They were mostly aware, for example, that masculinity influencers wanted to make money from them, and presented exaggerated personas for shock value. But the boys did also reveal some worrying attitudes that seemed to come straight from the manosphere: that men are now at a disadvantage in society, that women may say they want equality but secretly prefer a dominant and controlling man, and that women use their sexuality to get ahead.

At first sight, the boys' knowledge that they are being manipulated and their susceptibility to repeating such negative gender stereotypes seem contradictory. We think the answer lies in the insecurity many boys and young men feel – whether that relates to relationships with women, their economic future or what it means to be a man in the world right now. The messages boys see online offer them easy solutions for these anxieties. Online misogynists co-opt this vulnerability to preach that women are to blame. We need to bear this in mind when considering how best to undermine their influence.

Having talked to some boys, we now needed to find out what the girls and young women coming of age in the era of online misogyny are thinking. What are their experiences, and do they feel enough is being done to tackle these harms? Let's head over to hear from the girls.

Chapter 5

Girls Talking

So let's turn to the young women of the UK who are at the sharp end of the explosion in online misogyny which prompted us to write this book in the first place. How are they experiencing a digital environment which seems increasingly dominated by divisive gender narratives? Are they aware of online misogyny, and how is their mental and physical well-being affected by it, if so? How do they feel about the boys and men in their lives as a result? To hear from young women first-hand, we interviewed girls aged between fifteen and twenty-one about their online interactions and the messages they were receiving about their place in society. We again recruited for our focus group via social media advertisements to gather a reasonably randomised sample. Unlike with the boys, however, where take-up was sluggish, we were inundated with applications from the moment our ads went live – an early indication of how passionate girls and young women are about this issue. They certainly told it to us straight, and our conversations took quite a different turn from those with the boys. Let's find out what Akua (twenty-one), Sana (seventeen), Annabel (sixteen), Sophia (seventeen) and Emmy (fifteen), all either school or university students, had to say.

> *'I don't think that I want to be interacting with the type of content I'm seeing on the general feed. So, I'm going to lower the amount of time that I spend on it.'* – ***Akua, twenty-one***

As with the boys, we began by asking the girls about their habitual digital usage: how much time did they generally spend online in a day, and on which platforms. Their responses more or less mirrored the boys'. Sana's response was fairly typical: 'I will use my phone as an alarm clock and then scroll on it a bit to wake up. I'd then use it sometimes throughout the school day. In my school, phones are banned unless you're in the sixth-form designated zones. So, I'd use my phone then, and quite a bit after school. I rely on social media as my main form of communication. So, I'd probably speak to people on apps like Instagram, Snapchat, and I use LinkedIn and YouTube a lot as well.'

It's a familiar roll-call, of course, echoed by Annabel: 'I mostly use TikTok, Instagram and Snapchat, and I use them in school sometimes when I have a free period. I use TikTok in the evening and Snapchat to text my friends and stuff like that.'

For those still in school, using phones during the school day was pretty accepted. Sophia told us, 'My school does let us use phones in school, but it's generally not recommended to use them in class, obviously. So in free periods my friends will be scrolling through TikTok or having a bit of a laugh over that. Once I've done all my homework after school, I tend to just open my phone, reply to all my friends and what they've said. I use Snapchat, TikTok, Instagram as well. Snapchat again mostly for texting friends and TikTok mostly for fun and sending videos.'

For Emmy (fifteen), phones were out of bounds at school: 'I normally just use my phone maybe a little bit in the morning before school and then probably after it. And I have Instagram and TikTok and Snapchat. And I only really use Snapchat to talk to my friends.'

Some of the girls we spoke to were more active than the boys in actually creating content and posting on social media. Sophia, for example, told us, 'I would say that most people, most teenagers at least, are more consumers rather than posters that I've come across. But I do post on Instagram. I do post on TikTok sometimes as well. I have private accounts, but I do also have public ones. When I do post, it's mostly things like events, things that have happened. And it's not a daily thing that I would say is part of my life.'

The majority, though, posted little. Protecting their privacy quickly emerged as a concern – something which didn't come to the fore in our interviews with the boys. Sana said, 'None of my accounts are public. I tend to just consume media. I don't tend to post actively on those platforms.' Akua agreed: 'I'm more of a consumer than a poster.'

Annabel, the most active poster among the girls, had taken steps to preserve her online anonymity: 'I have two accounts on Instagram, one private and one public. And I post on the private one. On TikTok, I used to have two accounts. I have a private account, but I also had an anonymous account to post about political stuff and world events, where people could comment.' Emmy, the youngest of the girls, also kept a low public profile on social media: 'I'm definitely more of a consumer. I have posted on Instagram, but very rarely. And all of my accounts are private as well.'

> *'I think it's very easy for people to start spreading negative things and then for an algorithm to just force you more.'* ***–Emmy, fifteen***

As with the boys, some of the girls expressed the view that social media was becoming an unpleasant space, leading them to take steps to restrict time spent there. When asked how long she spent on it a day, Akua told us, 'I'd say a maximum of two hours. I think that that's the max. A lot of it goes to random internet searches for readings and stuff for university. And then sometimes some scrolling, but it was definitely worse before. Because of how toxic social media has gotten, I've actually made those changes to be like, "I don't think that I want to be interacting with the type of content I'm seeing on the general feed. So, I'm going to lower the amount of time that I spend on it."'

Emmy was also monitoring time spent on her phone, and worried that it was excessive: 'It definitely goes up at the weekend, but I'd say a maximum of three hours, which is something that I want to decrease. I just don't think it's very good to be consuming so much quick media and a lot of negative things as well.'

Like Adrian in the last chapter, Sana was worried about the effect of short-form video content like TikTok on her attention span. She was also trying to cut down: 'I've tried to stop consuming this kind of quick media. I'd say my screen time averages about six hours, seven hours daily, but I think only about two hours of that is on social media. And if it's more, it tends to be not consuming media, but instead using platforms like Instagram and Snapchat to message friends and to have conversations. I do consciously try when using my phone to watch long-form content, and to try and watch educational videos or use it to listen to music and other digitally enriched areas of my life, rather than just focusing on social media because I think it has very negative consequences and is quite toxic at times.'

The girls didn't always find social media scrolling an enjoyable activity. Much as was the case with the boys, it became clear that they found themselves being bombarded with divisive content, including online misogyny, with the algorithm pushing it into their feeds even when they didn't engage with it. Emmy told us, 'I think it's very easy for people to start spreading negative things and then for an algorithm to just force you more. If I see one video about one thing, then lots of videos will also come about the same thing, and it's not something that I necessarily want to be seeing.' She continued, 'I think social media a lot of the time can be quite desensitised because anyone can just post anything at any time. Sometimes the way the algorithms work can be quite damaging too.'

Akua highlighted the polarising, sometimes extremist, views which users feel emboldened to express on social media, and which, it often seems, are amplified by the algorithm: 'You never really get a balance. You often get like a person who's like, "I don't think that women should be able to work," and that's the view that you get the most. Political debates can become quite toxic because extremist views are being platformed that we're constantly having to shut down, and it's really hard when it's constantly coming at you over and over again.'

The girls we spoke to were mostly actively curating their feeds to see more of what interested them, but reported that, even when consuming content they found engaging, such as other women's accounts posting about success or feminist issues, the comments section was often a hotbed of personal attacks and misogyny. Akua explained, 'So, it can be a post about the Green Party [which she supports] and then you'll see a list of like antisemitic comments, or even a woman posting that she just graduated and then you just see a string of misogynistic comments in the comments section.'

She told us that she found this upsetting and continued, 'I'm not getting a flush of posts that are from the far right or from misogynists, but the fact is that it's seeping into the regular content that I watch. I have to always block the comments section and not look at it. And sometimes people will link to other videos that are just extreme far-right misogynists, that are also racist, and that will sometimes just say the worst things. It's like an entire conversation happening in the comments that is really toxic, and people constantly having to fight back against it. I saw someone who's a black woman and very successful in her career, and then as soon as you see the comments it's like, "oh, diversity hire". It's really disheartening when you see those types of things.'

Sophia agreed: 'When I do have more feminist things coming up on my page, there will be often be a very harsh atmosphere in the comments replying to it, trying to obliterate not only the argument, but the person that's actually saying, "You know, guys, maybe this isn't a good thing." It'll be more like an attack on their personality or their looks. They'll go on their profile and be like: "Well, actually, I don't think you're attractive, so you shouldn't say something" – when it's completely unrelated.'

When we asked what the girls thought was driving these attacks on women, Sana ventured, 'I think it's important to say that it seems as though lots of things are up for debate now when they really shouldn't be. There's an argument that everything needs to be considered from both sides as opposed to quite frankly saying, well, women need equal rights. Women should not be treated in this way. I think the rise of social media has definitely impacted that. It feels like because there is so much free speech and so many unmoderated platforms, that everything suddenly warrants an opinion.'

Sophia was thoughtful, expressing an understanding that attitudes promoted by powerful influencers had trickled down to shape wider social media culture: 'A few years ago, the main figure was Andrew Tate. That has very much passed now with everything that happened, but I don't think we can really pin this to one person or one movement as much any more because it's become so holistic. It's become part of the culture. When you scroll down it's not going to be one person on a podcast saying a specific thing. It'll be normal people just posting things. Your average guy in secondary school will post a [misogynistic] TikTok. It will just be a normal person, not an influencer or a big figure. And that shows how ingrained it's become.'

> *'They're like, "Oh, it's just for laughs. I'm just trying to make you mad," but it's not really a joke, though.'* – ***Sophia, seventeen***

As we chatted to the girls more about where they felt exposed to misogyny, they told us that boys at school and uni often sent them misogynistic jokes, memes and links to content denigrating or humiliating women. Sophia told us, 'I would say when I have come across misogynistic content, it's because it's sent to me by boys sometimes. So, I go to a girls' secondary school and there's quite a posh boys' school down the road and I interact with them for clubs and cadets and things like that, and a lot of the time they'll send me things that come up on their pages. It'll be quite sexist, and I'll be like, "Why are you sending me this? I never implied that this would be okay." And they're like, "Oh, it's just for laughs. I'm just trying to make you mad," but it's not really a joke, though.'

All the girls we spoke to recognised this 'banter culture': boys target girls with toxic ideas about women parroted from social media, while benefiting from the plausible deniability of saying they are only joking, making it difficult to hold them accountable. Sana explained, 'I know people [at school] who will be very disrespectful and very rude and maybe make snide comments towards women. Kind of like rape culture jokes, but interwoven with Snapchat stickers and a few emojis. And so I think that social media isn't only helping people to feel more confident in saying things, but also working to diminish the impact and the horrors of what they are actually thinking.'

She continued: 'This idea of rage-baiting becomes the only real way to gain social currency. In political discussions I think it happens very frequently that men lean towards trying to represent issues that are actually harmful to women because it makes them seem interesting, and then they're able to use this excuse afterwards to say, "Oh well clearly I don't agree with this. I'm just playing a part."'

Sana is articulating here what it feels like to be on the receiving end of the 'rage-bait' banter which Adam referred to as boys saying things for effect and 'playing devil's advocate' in the last chapter.

We asked the girls whether they felt able to have open conversations with any of the boys in their lives about issues of sexism and how it affected them. Sophia felt this was difficult as boys didn't tend to take it seriously: 'I go to a girls' school, and they were trying to get an initiative together with the boys' school for PSHE to make sure that they crack down on sexism and have a plan moving forwards. I was telling my friends about it in the boys' school and they said, "Oh yeah, we definitely need that." I said, "Why are you so certain that we need it?" And they were like, "Because we're so sexist." And I was like, "Well, you're telling me this, so you're aware of it, but you're not doing anything about it. What's going on there?"' She continued, 'I think it's because no boy believes they're sexist, because "Well, women have equal pay and are equal to men in law so sexism isn't a problem any more."'

At Sana's school, the boys did not engage with the limited time devoted to learning about gender discrimination in PSHE: 'They said that they couldn't identify with the issues that they were being taught. A lot of them were saying, "Well, how does this affect us?" and, "It doesn't affect us at all, so why should we be learning about it?" Our teachers emphasised that, of course, the patriarchy impacts men negatively as well, but they still didn't care.'

The girls did, however, report some positive and nuanced discussions with male friends and relatives about the impact of misogyny on them. Annabel said, 'I had a good conversation with a male friend of mine. We were at a party together and people were making comments which came from an online trend. If you're on TikTok, I think you'll know. It was something along the lines of "Get back in the kitchen" or "When she finally makes me a sandwich, I don't need to hit her." So, we had a really good conversation about where it comes from and how I see it from my perspective – about how what is seen as one quick joke, which lasts a second, keeps reinforcing ideas. It keeps getting regurgitated into classrooms and social settings and we talked about how it starts online but moves its way into everyday life.'

Akua told us about a conversation with her younger brother: 'He's sixteen. So, he tells me, "This is what boys at school are saying," and, "This is what my friends send me." He's often expressed that he's very confused by the manosphere and where it came from. And he's watched *Adolescence* as well. He even said that it was really confusing to him that other boys in school were telling him, "Oh, okay, you know, women are this, women are that, we'd be happier if women were in more traditional gender roles." Hearing his side of the story and him saying, "I don't agree with this at all, but I'm really confused. What should I believe?" was really positive.'

All the girls we spoke to felt that their schools needed to do more to tackle misogyny and educate boys and girls about its effects. Akua felt she had to take it upon herself to learn about how sexism operates in society: 'Year Seven, I think, I definitely started to question, "Okay, why am I seeing these differences between the way that boys and girls are treated?" and I started to explore the sixth-form library in school, which is where I first picked up bell hooks, first picked up Virginia Woolf, and then that's really how it started. I founded the Feminist Society in Year Eight with some of my teachers because I saw the way that girls were treated at school and I was like, "I think this should become an issue that we talk about in school." But it was definitely self-directed. I had some citizenship lessons about it, but if you really wanted to delve deep into it, you had to choose sociology at A level, which I chose, but a lot of people didn't.'

Sana had a similar experience: 'In school it's been a fight to do more self-directed learning to try and understand misogyny. I think that within the PSHE curriculum, especially in my school (and I don't know if this is just a "my school" thing or a grammar school thing in general), there's been a move away from long sessions for PSHE to just a few form-time activities. So twenty minutes in the morning and then a whole day of PSHE when you can get it.'

For Annabel, 'I'd say we only had maybe fifteen minutes at the start of a PSHE lesson, but in my school, a lot of debates about this came from actual class debates of issues that arose in class. So if a boy made a comment about a cover teacher, the teacher stopped the class, we'd have a discussion about it. So that's where most of my education towards that came from.'

Emmy felt that her school was actively shutting down any debate on the pervasive ideology of the online manosphere: 'I think we have touched upon feminism and misogyny in PSHE, but I do think it has been very surface level. A few years ago when Andrew Tate was quite big, we had an assembly where they said, "You are not allowed to talk about Andrew Tate. If we hear you talk about it, you'll be punished." And it was quite a severe punishment. It was like isolation or suspension. But while I do see how they just didn't want anyone idolising him, I thought that was actually quite negative because no one could talk about it. If no one could talk about it, no one could share their experiences or say how it was negative. It was just very hushed up. And I don't think that that was the right way to deal with it.'

We've reported elsewhere in the book on the evidence that boys are using misogynist beliefs learned online to target female teachers with harassment. Concerningly, the girls confirmed this to be the case from their own experience. They told us about teachers being on the receiving end of sexist and dismissive comments from boys. Sophia said, 'The way that boys talk about their teachers sometimes is something that I think needs to be explored. For example, in my school, there was a cover teacher who was a plus-size model and they were absolutely horrible to her. They sexualise women. Whenever female teachers try to talk about sexism, they just laugh about it because, "It's taking time out of our day, we'd rather be playing football."'

> *'I feel like there is definitely a trend of some people saying, "I hate men." But I haven't seen this translated into real life in the same way that misogyny will have the effect of femicide, women being raped, being killed.'* – ***Akua, twenty-one***

Perhaps unsurprisingly, unlike the boys, the girls all understood the working definitions of 'misogyny' and 'patriarchy'. They also appeared somewhat frustrated by how feminism was being represented online. We asked them how they felt about the argument that it had gone too far, and that men were now being targeted by women with 'misandrist' attitudes. Some of the girls agreed that 'anti-male' sentiment existed in online spaces, but argued that since it lacked the systemic and structural power of misogyny, it was more of a defence mechanism from women, or a reaction to their personal experiences at the hands of men.

Here is Sophia again: 'Women a lot of the time say, "I hate men. They've done this, this, this, this, this. They're annoying." The idea of a gender war comes into play. But a lot of the time what they're saying is grounded in completely real and valid experiences.'

Akua noted that misandry, or hatred of men, did not generally result in the risk of violence for men: 'I think patriarchy is a system and misandry is a reaction. Sometimes I've noticed that some people will try to make misandry out to be the same thing as misogyny. I don't think that that's the case. I think that when people say, for example, "I hate men," men will react to that and say, "Why do you hate men?" or "Why are you saying all men?" Usually we're not saying all men. We're seeing enough to be able to say, "Okay, this is an issue among men." I feel like there is definitely a trend of some people saying, "I hate men." But I haven't seen this translated into real life in the same way that misogyny has will have the effect of femicide, women being raped, being killed. I haven't seen misandry have that effect on men. Maybe some people would feel hurt by women saying, "I hate men." But it just hasn't had the impact that misogyny has had for millennia.'

Annabel was also clearly opposed to the idea that misandry was equivalent to misogyny: 'A lot of the time misandry is a form of defence because whenever women try to go online and start a conversation about an issue like violence, or femicide or how women's abuse isn't taken seriously, men will sometimes take over the conversation and get on the defensive. So women talk about how after football matches rates of domestic violence go up, and then men might turn it into #NotAllMen, and then it becomes quite a male-dominated conversation.* Like a few weeks or months ago there was a question: "Would you rather be alone in the woods with a man or a bear?" which should have been quite a good conversation about how women feel unsafe around half of society.† But it [the debate] turned to men's feelings – men getting defensive that people think of them that way.'

Emmy had also followed the man vs bear discussion play out on social media and felt 'it could have been an opportunity for women to explain their fears associated with men, and how they would feel safer being alone with a bear at night rather than a man. But I think that was met with a lot of outrage [from men], like, "Oh, that's ridiculous. You couldn't say that – a bear would kill you instantly." Just a lot of dismissiveness rather than actually trying to understand where they were coming from.'

Despite this, the girls were aware that women's online anger about misogyny could alienate boys and men. As we saw from the last chapter, feminist arguments do not necessarily resonate with them. Sophia felt that online debates need to be de-escalated if men are to be engaged positively with women's fight for equality: 'I think maybe what we [women and girls] need to start doing is to remove that dismissive tone to men, considering that their reaction to this is to be, you know, insecure. If we remove that from our language, then hopefully they'll remove that from theirs.'

Our discussion of how boys might be 'turned off' feminism turned to the currently popular TikTok trope of influencers

* #NotAllMen is a popular hashtag used by men in online conversations about violence against women and girls.
† The question was sparked by a video by TikTokker @callmebkbk in 2024.

mocking men who claim to be feminists as 'performative males', and expressing the belief that they are doing so solely as a manipulation tactic to achieve popularity with women.[1]

Sana felt the mockery was sometimes justified since, in her eyes, some men did attempt to use a professed interest in feminism to ingratiate themselves with women. She referred to 'this trend in trying to pursue romantic relationships where people are: "Oh, here's all my feminist literature, I'm so wonderful. I love women's rights. I hate period cramps." They are just trying to satirise real women's issues. You're not actually going to read feminist literature, are you? There's a layer underneath that's quite malicious, and I really don't like that.'

However, all the girls disliked the term, which is used by both men and women on TikTok, claiming that it makes boys even less likely to identify as feminist. In Emmy's words: 'I think lots of boys my age are really scared of being seen as feminist, especially with this rise online of being a "performative male". They don't necessarily want to come across as being sexist but they don't want to be seen as feminist either. I think they have a very wrong idea of feminism. They're all like, "Oh, yeah, girl power," but that's not really what feminism is.'

Sana felt men's support needed to be more authentic: 'Obviously men have the responsibility to ask about how they can better support women, but it shouldn't be just this idea of wearing feminism as a badge; something that you use to show off. It shouldn't be used like a cultural differentiator, rather than a means of creating a better and more tolerant society.'

> *'There's been a change and a shift. Girls now are more accepting of not going to university, not getting a career.'* – ***Sophia, seventeen***

The girls were keen to tell us more about how harmful online narratives were reaching into their lives, and some of these surprised us. Several, for example, shared their opinion that female-coded subjects at school, such as humanities and the arts, are being systematically devalued in some viral social media content. The girls felt this was spilling over into their real-life experiences at school and university.

Annabel, for example, said that, in her experience, 'subjects that a lot of girls go into, like history and humanities subjects in my school, are seen as easier and less valid subjects. And now we're beginning to talk more about university, a lot of girls I know want to do history degrees, law degrees and anthropology. And when we talk about it in group settings of boys, these are seen as easy cop-out degrees – almost like "Mickey Mouse" degrees people have called them. A lot of the time degrees which are more women-dominated are seen as easier and have less value.'

Sophia agreed: 'It seems that there's become some kind of hierarchy of degrees and career path, which is horrible to think about because surely academia in its entirety should be celebrated.'

Akua acknowledged that at her university, 'I am definitely living in that hierarchy of degrees where the people who do economics or the people who do STEM do feel a sense of superiority over people who do humanities,' and she referred to economic insecurity as a contributing factor: 'There is an increasing fear because of youth unemployment. At the moment a lot of us uni students are scared. Even though I'm only in my first year, we are scared about what will happen after, so subjects that are typically seen as more feminine, some people will be like, "Oh yeah, me doodling and doing my little arts degree while he does his big boy STEM degree," which I've seen on TikTok over and over again.'

The girls had all noticed an uptick on social media in content promoting the value of more socially conservative roles for women in society, such as the rapidly growing 'trad wife' subculture. On Instagram and TikTok, perfectly groomed female influencers post hundreds of videos focused on cooking, cleaning, gardening and caring for their families, showcasing an often explicit narrative that women are happier at home.[2]

Sophia felt this trend should also be considered in its socio-economic context with increasing unemployment and the high cost of living leaving many young people struggling to find good jobs and financial security: 'Obviously I can't speak for everyone, but I think there's been a fear, especially among women, of "What is going to be my economic future?" And I think some people see that and think, "I can't possibly try to fight my way through this impossible structure ahead of me. Surely it would be easier just to not get a career and maybe settle down as a housewife," which I think is sad.'

Akua felt the 'trad wife' trend was being instrumentalised by the American conservative right wing, among others, to stigmatise women's educational and career ambitions: 'I've noticed a trend on social media where you'll have, for example, a woman posting that she's just graduated or she's going to university and a man will comment: "You'd be much more suited to being in the kitchen," or, "The workplace is never going to fulfil you."'

She went on, 'When Charlie Kirk was alive, that was the rhetoric that we saw everywhere – that no job is going to fulfil you.* It's only going to be being a wife and having children. Or him telling young girls, "If you're going to college, you should actually be going to college to find a husband." There was a term for it – "MRS" degree. They called a woman going to university, getting a degree, a "MRS" degree. And I feel that's really concerning because some women seeing this content may start to be convinced that working or having an education isn't important any more, and that they won't be appealing [to men] if they want to go after these things, and that they won't be able to have a satisfying relationship or have children and also be able to have an education, work and express their opinions freely.'

Akua, a practising Christian, and Sana, a practising Muslim, both noted how manosphere beliefs interacted with their specific cultural and religious backgrounds. Akua was concerned by 'the rise in America of this very misogynistic form of Christianity which has told women, "You should stay at home, don't get an education, don't speak up, be submissive." And it's really scary to me that this is becoming a dominant theme. In recent years we're seeing these people who are alt-right extreme conservatives, who are also extremely racist, extremely homophobic, transphobic, and it's just really scary that now you see them all over social media. They're spreading this very hateful rhetoric that isn't Christianity at all.'

Sana reflected on this tendency to police women among some in her own religious community: 'I don't know about other religions, but I assume there will be quite similar alpha male

* Charlie Kirk was an American conservative activist and commentator best known as the founder and president of Turning Point USA. He was murdered in October 2025.

podcasters. I know in Islam that is a really big thing, with people trying to push this idea of the "haram police". Trying to stick to these ideas of what a woman should be and how she should conform and what's expected for a wife as though being a wife is this ultimate thing.' Sana felt that to tackle misogyny effectively, attempts by parents and educators needed to take a culturally sensitive approach: 'I think it comes back to trying to find a more intersectional approach to deconstructing the manosphere, because what's going to work on one boy is going to be completely different to somebody else raised in a different culture.'

> *'Trying to create this kind of welcoming atmosphere would be lovely.'* – ***Sana, seventeen***

We asked the girls what advice they'd most like to give to the parents and carers reading this book. They had some considered thoughts on this topic, but stressed, above all, the need for early intervention at home as essential to raising boys and girls as equals.

Here is Akua: 'I think that conversations should be had early on. If you leave it only up to schools to teach your children that "this isn't a way to treat women" or that "misogyny is bad", once they get home after school with their friends, what is their family community like? That can impact a child a lot. And if they are in a family where misogynistic comments get thrown around – even if it's not directly to the child, but they overhear it – that can impact them a lot, and sometimes they'll end up bringing it to school as well and you start seeing issues.'

Emmy agreed, telling us, 'I do think this is something that needs to be stopped at a young age. And I think education is really important and talking about what makes a good role model for men, and knowing how misogyny and patriarchy are ingrained in society. Being able to have conversations with children about it is really important, because as boys grow older they draw apart from their parents a bit.'

Sophia echoed this, emphasising the need to break down gender stereotypes. She said, 'I think that for parents it's having those conversations early, and fostering an environment that is anti-sexist and openly talks about misogyny. When a child is younger, it's very important to be able to have that discussion. But also, not to see your child as, "Oh, because she's a girl, I'm going to do this; because he's a boy, I'm going to do this." That's definitely not okay. Also, the idea that the father teaches the son, the mother teaches the daughter – really it should be integrated into the structure of the family. We shouldn't have these defined gender roles, meaning that only the father can talk to the son about specific things, or only the mother can talk to the daughter about specific things. I think that's something that needs to be completely done away with.'

Sana had some suggestions as to how families could tackle sexist norms at home: 'Even simple fixes like reading your male children books marketed for girls, or books with heroines, rather than heroes, seeing movies with more women in them and, even with your personal anecdotes, not always using "he" as the default gender. Instead, trying to create a welcoming atmosphere would be lovely.'

These comments demonstrate an awareness among the girls that the online and real-world misogyny they are subjected to daily is rooted in wider norms, including within the family. They stand in sharp contrast to some of the boys' more essentialist views on gender difference. This may reflect the varying digital echo chambers inhabited by girls and boys or, more likely, the fact that experiences of sexism have prompted the girls to a more in-depth analysis of the issue.

As we closed the focus group discussion, Emmy offered one final observation: 'The idea that boys and girls can't be friends [is] definitely something that we need to change.'

The poignancy of this last simple wish caused us both to stop and think. If even the simple and basic human joy of friendship is something boys and girls feel they need to reclaim, isn't it time urgently to reassess the world they are growing up in? That world, to a greater and greater extent, is the digital one, so let's head to it now to find out where our boys are hanging out, and what they are learning there about men, women, masculinity, sex and power.

Chapter 6

Boys Behind Screens

From the conversations we had with friends and family while writing this book, it has certainly struck us how little parents, and adults in general, actually know about their teens' and children's digital hangouts. The interviews in the preceding chapters show that the algorithmic 'personalisation' of social media, which predicts what will compel users to spend the most time on their platforms, is leading to very different experiences of the internet for boys and for girls.

While girls may be immersed in the polished perfection and seductive poses of filtered Instagram selfies posted by celebrities and influencers, and subsequently feel the pressure to look and behave similarly, they are also exposed to some more empowering messages about feminism and women's rights to self-expression. A quick glance at Amelia's niece's Instagram feed, for example, reveals that a stream of fashion, hairstyling and dance videos is peppered with funny and inspirational posts from accounts such as the Girls Groupchat (7.5 million followers across platforms) which encourage girls' friendship, independence and ambition.

But girls' social media consumption, as confirmed in the previous chapter's interviews, also includes some divisive messaging around heterosexual relationships and dating, such as that men who call themselves feminists are just 'performative'. The gurus of the manosphere preach that men and women cannot possibly form a partnership of equals since to be truly 'alpha', a man must dominate and control his partner. It also ruthlessly reduces women to two stereotypes: 'traditionally' feminine-submissive and mercenary-promiscuous. With the rise of digital 'dating coaches', some of the content that girls themselves view on a regular basis reinforces damaging gender stereotypes in a different way, reframing them as female empowerment.

TikTok trends such as 'princessing' and the 'boyfriend test', for example, where women ask their partners to perform more and more demanding services for them, can set unrealistic expectations for all genders about what is normal behaviour in relationships.[1]

This content risks offering men confirmation of the messaging, pushed by harmful influencers, that women's attitude to men is entirely transactional. Just like the 'men going their own way' misogynists we followed in Chapter Three, some young women even appear ready to eschew heterosexual dating altogether, a phenomenon widespread enough to have spawned the term 'heterofatalism'.[2] An American podcast aimed at young women, *Delusional Diaries*, recently hosted a conversation on whether having a boyfriend is now 'uncool'. Commenters on Instagram expressed opinions on the episode which included describing being with a man as 'basically charity' and how boyfriends are 'out of style' and wouldn't be fashionable again until they behaved better.[3]

A lot of dating advice is fairly innocuous and many young people find it helpful. But some at the more polarised end of this content spectrum may be feeding the apparently growing gender hostility among younger generations. As we've seen, girls and boys have historically often had different interests, reinforced by gender expectations. Girls are socialised into shopping and beauty treatments, boys into team sports and cars, for example. But, prior to the age of the algorithm, most leisure and cultural experiences were generally shared across gender groups. When Amelia was a teen, the weekend group cinema visit was a rite of passage, and everyone at school listened to the Top 40 on Radio 1 every Sunday and went to the youth club on Friday night. For Matteo, friend groups gathered at the local park to chill, MTV was a staple, as was burning CDs of your favourite music.

To a degree we have now lost some of the shared cultural trends that united previous generations. As we've seen, boys' and girls' cultural consumption can be vastly different. Online echo chambers mean that we all end up seeing a much narrower view of the world tailored to our specific preferences, a world where the perspectives the algorithm calculates will engage us are amplified and those which reflect different interests or views may never find us. So, let's ask the question, do you know exactly, or even approximately, what the boys and young men in your life are looking at online? Let's take a closer look.

Like. Comment. Subscribe.

For both of us when we were growing up, watching certain TV shows was non-negotiable if you wanted to join in with break-time chat at school – what we used to call 'water-cooler moments'. For Amelia, *Top of the Pops* and *Blackadder* were required viewing, whereas for Matteo, *High School Musical* and episodes of *Friends* were keenly dissected, and slang and jokes from MTV and *Pimp my Ride* adopted in the playground. You needed to understand these shared references to retain any playground clout. As young people's media consumption habits have transformed with the internet and smartphone usage, this experience of bonding over shared TV viewing has declined. However, that does not mean that children and young people are not watching video content. Quite the reverse.

In 2024, 98 per cent of thirteen- to fifteen-year-olds used video-sharing platforms, rising to 99 per cent for sixteen- to seventeen-year-olds. For children of all ages in the UK, YouTube is overwhelmingly the most popular online space, and the one with the youngest user profile, used by 84 per cent of three- to seventeen-year-olds.[4] YouTube and YouTube Shorts (its short-form, vertical video site, rolled out in 2021 as a direct response to the surging popularity of TikTok) are particularly widely used by boys and young men. A 2025 survey found that 77 per cent of boys aged eleven to seventeen watched YouTube *daily*.[5] The most watched video content among boys is made up of a mix of funny and 'prank' videos, sports commentary, and gaming walkthroughs.[6] This closely corresponds to what Amelia knew of the online activities of her own Gen Z son, PJ, now an adult, so she spoke to him about what he remembered of his digital life as a younger boy to find out more about the appeal of this content.

PJ confirmed that YouTube featured in his earliest access to the internet as a child, even before acquiring his own mobile phone at the age of eleven, since the family iPad was available for him to use after school, even as his gaming console had (ironically) been designated off-limits in a bid by his parents to reduce screen time. His memories of his online habits backed up some of what we heard from the boys in Chapter Four: passive viewing of streamed gaming content, prank videos and funny viral clips. PJ also had a ringside seat for the rapid rise to fame of the professional YouTuber, and some of his preferred YouTube influencers remain among the UK's biggest entertainment stars.

The Sidemen, for example, started unofficially around 2014 as a group of young gaming streamers who loosely collaborated on clips and challenges. Now, their members, unofficially led by the rapper and boxer KSI (aka Olajide Olayinka Williams Olatunji), have more than 155 million shared subscribers and preside over a multimillion-pound content creation empire. Their output has expanded to include game shows, reality TV, dating and travel formats, clothing lines, and sporting challenges to raise funds for mental health charities.[7] If there is such a thing as water-cooler TV for Gen Z boys and men, the most popular Sidemen videos are probably it. At the time of writing, the most recent episode of a regular feature, 20 Women vs 1 Sidemen, currently stands at 8.1 million views on YouTube. Many struggling terrestrial broadcasters could only ever dream of such numbers.

When, in 2023, KSI collaborated with US YouTuber and boxer Logan Paul (who he had fought five years earlier in a hugely hyped boxing match) to market a new 'sports' drink, Prime, demand rapidly outstripped supply among fans. Some news reports at the time suggested that bottles were changing hands among fans for upwards of £100.[8] The likes of the Sidemen, Logan Paul and his brother Jake, DanTDM, Mr Beast, Ali-A and the controversial PewDiePie loomed large in PJ's media consumption as a young teen and remain some of the most powerful online voices, with content specifically targeted to appeal to the interests of their young, overwhelmingly male fanbase.

The near ubiquitous use of YouTube and the star power of its top creators has spawned the nearest many young men find these days to a community of like-minded companions. The comments sections of popular videos show viewers enjoying the content together, sharing their reactions and how they relate to it in ways that feel genuinely sociable. Experts have noted that ardent followers of online influencers may demonstrate 'para-social' feelings for them, investing emotionally in a relationship which is, in reality, purely one-sided.[9] When this ardent fandom prompts scuffles in supermarkets among young people desperate to buy a bottle of relentlessly hyped fizzy water, it can perhaps be brushed off as a clever marketing ploy by a new generation of media celebrities. However, some other voices which have risen to fame on YouTube have more malevolent, though just as mercenary, intentions.

Amelia's son PJ admits that some of the content he viewed on YouTube as a child, posted by his favourite influencers, was not always age-appropriate and some was offensive: he referred specifically to bad language and racial slurs. KSI, for example, has repeatedly used sexist and racist language in his content, including rape jokes (which he has since apologised for).[10] This was a source of conflict between Amelia and the teenage PJ, and looking back, she regrets not paying more attention to the amount of time her son was spending in the company of these random companions and some of the more dubious content they promoted. PJ admitted that from around the age of fourteen or fifteen, his YouTube feed would tend to feature, alongside the prank and gaming videos he preferred, more divisive, even hostile content pitting young men like himself against other, specific groups. In his words these videos showed 'feminists and queer people, transgender people, being "owned", made to look like crazy people'.

Some of the names regularly posting this content we've come across before, like Sneako and Myron Gaines, host of the *Fresh and Fit* podcast, but others mentioned by PJ, like Ben Shapiro and Steven Crowder, are more associated with the 'radical conservatism' wing of American politics and profess what would generally be considered extreme views, including opposing abortion and same-sex marriage; Crowder believes that a woman should not be allowed to divorce without her husband's permission unless she can prove wrongdoing by him.[11] Many studies have shown that, regardless of whether they search for it or not, algorithms on video-sharing platforms are recommending misogynist content to young men, with one finding it took only twenty-six minutes on YouTube for a sixteen- to eighteen-year-old male 'sock puppet' user account to be served videos by 'manfluencers' such as the ones we met in Chapter Three.[12] PJ confessed that the content he viewed as a young teen, 'definitely made me feel more anti-"woke". Personally speaking, I wasn't turned against all feminists. But I feel like most men would definitely be turned against feminism by that.'

YouTube is one of several online platforms that profits from users' desire to follow popular content trends. But there is now mounting evidence that, for some boys, by serving them bridging content, which they may consider edgy or funny, it is also leading them down a steep algorithmic slope to consuming more and more extreme material, including much which is openly misogynistic.

'How to Stop Being a Nice Guy'

'I was kind of isolated in school. I was the lonely kid. I was the outsider. I had a very hard time making friends.' In 2020, as schools closed and the UK went into lockdown to mitigate the spread of Covid-19, Calum Jackson, fourteen, found himself entirely bereft of social contact for a period of many months. A shy teen with autism, he took solace in the online world and the brashly confident voices he found there.

The SOUK programmes team had been following Calum for a while on TikTok, where he'd been posting frankly about his descent into extremism and subsequent journey of deradicalisation. We made contact with him to gather insights for our PCVE (preventing and countering violent extremism) work and he was generous enough to talk to us about his experience of having his world view radically changed by the content he discovered on YouTube. Now nineteen and happily studying Economics at university, he explains: 'I didn't actively go out searching for a lot of this content. It just kind of appeared on my feed over time. It slowly crept its way in.'

As Amelia's son PJ noted earlier, 'anti-woke' content which showcases manosphere tropes is a staple of some young men's feeds, and PJ admitted that it affected his own views as a teen. But while most boys may be content to shrug this stuff off as 'banter' or see through it entirely, for others, finding a handy scapegoat for the issues that make them anxious has a stronger pull. Loneliness, a lack of economic and social opportunities, feeling unpopular with the opposite sex: all of these factors can predispose boys to identify with grievance narratives which misogynist creators are happy to validate. The Covid lockdown, when all of the above problems faced by young men were exacerbated, was the perfect breeding ground.

In his bedroom at home alone, and with no contact with kids his own age, Calum was served videos on YouTube from a podcast called the *Lotus Eaters*. The clips featured a collective of content creators including Carl Benjamin, a former member of the Eurosceptic political party UKIP, who gained notoriety in 2019 when standing to be a Member of the European Parliament for commenting that he 'wouldn't even rape' the MP Jess Phillips, and then adding the threat, 'I might cave.'[13] The *Lotus Eaters'* content explicitly blames feminism and immigration for the 'decline of the West', and showcases a variety of extreme right wing and misogynistic views, which appealed to Calum's lonely and embittered frame of mind at the time.[14] 'By the end of 2020, I'd very much been fully radicalised,' he confirms sadly.

The algorithmic pipeline rapidly funnelled Calum more of the same: videos from the *Whatever* podcast and the socially conservative creators of the Daily Wire, such as Ben Shapiro, who we met burning Barbie dolls, and he quickly found that misogyny was priced into the package: 'Anti-feminism, anti-LGBT views, and ethnic nationalism are very interlinked. The common overlap is the idea of decline prevalent in the hard right: the country used to be strong, but now we've just let woke overtake us and we've let the third world overrun us. This connects to the so-called great replacement theory* and the idea that feminism, LGBT, and disability awareness are making our society weak because men are supposed to be big strong stoic men for the strength of the nation,' Calum explains.

In a bid to become the dominant, masculine man his far-right ideology demanded, Calum sought out online advice to improve his physique and find the 'perfect' submissive woman touted as the ideal. The advice he received online began sensibly enough, covering topics like conversation skills, but quickly escalated to the 'red pill' narratives we've encountered before: 'Women are only attracted to bad boys and stereotypically masculine men. Nice guys finish last.' Calum learned from the likes of Hamza Ahmed and Andrew Tate that to get a girl he needed to conceal who he really was and cultivate a 'bad boy persona'.

Since Tate's widespread deplatforming and disgrace, Ahmed has emerged as a strong UK contender in the online misogyny ring. Boasting over 2 million subscribers on YouTube, he spouts classic 'red-pilled' talking points. These are mixed in with a smattering of psychobabble and dubious get-rich-quick advice in a pitch explicitly aimed at teenagers. A typical YouTube video boasts the title: 'If you're 16 to 22 years old, watch this.'

* A far-right, racist conspiracy theory which holds that there is a plot by elites to replace white populations in Western countries with non-white immigrants.

Calum confessed that he found Ahmed's content, though 'goofy in retrospect', 'so easy to fall for' as a fifteen- or sixteen-year-old, believing that success with women depended on maintaining 'a very rigid form of masculinity' to avoid being 'dumped or cheated on, or losing respect'. Ahmed's business empire, which includes courses on 'how to get girls without being weird or creepy' and promises to make boys 'ready to dominate', monetises teenage boys' normal insecurities.[15] In most of his videos, he rants at his followers, chastising them for laziness and 'degeneracy' (usually used to mean gaming and masturbation) and exhorting them to follow his advice in order to become a chisel-jawed 'Adonis' (Ahmed's version of a 'Chad').

As Calum has now recognised, much of Ahmed's content is truly cringeworthy. Having watched them, we can confirm that his '17 Laws of Masculinity' are exhaustive, and surely an *exhausting* prospect for any young man.

Yet Ahmed's following is so devoted that it has cultish undertones. Typical comments on his videos include, 'You've been that older brother figure to me,' and, 'Hamza is the masculine father we all need.' James Blake's documentary *Men of the Manosphere* (2025) tracked the story of one Hamza Ahmed devotee, Sam, who had renounced all his friends and left school at sixteen to follow his guru's path and become an online influencer himself.

As we've observed elsewhere, most of the lore of the manosphere does not bear much contact with reality. The 80/20 'hypergamy' theory unravelled for our interviewee, Calum, when he realised that most of his female relatives had apparently not ruled out marriage to men who lacked a granite jawline and millions in the bank. However, these narratives thrive when young men are isolated from real-world contact, so preaching that men need to shun their friends and family appears to be a calculated tactic.

Venom in the Voice Chat

Calum has now fully escaped the influence of the manosphere, and we'll explore how he did that later in the chapter. His indoctrination via YouTube is an example of how online extremists profit from the mechanisms of algorithmic optimisation to recruit boys and young men to harmful beliefs. Just like video-sharing sites, gaming platforms and gaming-adjacent chat rooms and streaming platforms such as Discord, Kick and Twitch are spaces used by the vast majority of boys on a daily basis. In fact, video gaming accounts for a high percentage of children's total time spent online, and the length of time playing is consistently higher for boys than girls across age groups.[16]

One recent report found that fifteen- to seventeen-year-old boys spend ninety-three minutes a day gaming.[17] It emerges from research (and from our own experience) as one of the recreational activities boys enjoy the most, with many parents saying their sons find it useful as a stress reliever and an important way to stay connected to friends and family.[18] As a teen, Amelia's son PJ gamed on a weekly basis with his cousin who lives at the other end of the country, cementing a strong friendship which has continued into adulthood (they still discuss their favourite *Destiny* 'raids' from years earlier). Matteo himself is a keen gamer to this day, and a big believer in its positive aspects.

Gaming with offline school friends is an almost universal pastime for boys in the UK; PJ felt that the screen time restrictions his parents put on gaming, no gaming on a school night, for example, actually inhibited his ability to build real-world friendships. Multiplayer games also provide a space where individuals can come together as teams (whether known to one another or not) to embark on shared challenges and activities which build important skills of communication and collaboration. Amelia sometimes jokes that while her son cannot find the milk carton in the fridge, he can spot an approaching sniper from five miles away when playing a first-person shooter game.

However, we do think it's essential for parents to be aware of some of the less positive aspects of these gaming environments. The emergence of online multiplayer games, many of which, such as Fortnite, Minecraft and Roblox, are hugely popular with children, also puts them in contact with older players they don't know in real life, and where they may encounter disturbing language and behaviour. When we discussed this with PJ and his cousin Alfie, they both confirmed that they routinely found themselves the targets of abuse by other players (often grown men) in multiplayer games. They laughingly dismissed the idea that they might have found this traumatising, with Alfie commenting in retrospect, 'It's not really threatening. I guess it's more people just insulting you and being like, "You're crap, blah, blah, blah." I remember me and PJ getting a load of messages on Xbox and people just being horrible to us, but I just sort of shrugged it off because it never really bothered me.'

PJ agreed: 'I was never really the victim of any kind of serious abuse that I can remember. I just feel like people would get annoyed and rage at you, but it would just be sort of an understood part of it.'

The boys' nonchalant dismissal of this online abuse as an accepted (and almost expected) aspect of gaming underscores its, somewhat self-cultivated, reputation as an entertainment form focused on the stereotypically male attributes of aggression and hyper-competitiveness. This is reflected in the data: witnessing toxic behaviour and discriminatory language is a common experience for boys while gaming. In 2025, 70 per cent of eleven- to seventeen-year-old boys had seen other players being bullied or harassed, 68 per cent had seen mean comments towards other players and 58 per cent had observed racist language. Only two in five boys had witnessed players actively standing up for those abused.[19]

Post-Gamergate, it is still undeniably true that the 'gamer' identity is closely tied to the traditional norms of masculinity we find in the 'man box', and that women players face hostility and abuse, both within games and as streamers.[20] This is reinforced, not only by the games themselves, which still often feature women as sexualised secondary characters, but by the attitudes of some of the most widely watched streamers, such as Sneako and Adin Ross, who are enthusiastic preachers of the manosphere.

Pokimane, the top female gaming influencer with over 9 million followers on Twitch, has repeatedly highlighted this, observing, in 2024, 'the rise of so much manosphere, red pill bullshit – I feel like that stuff has flourished within the male-dominated livestreaming sphere'.[21]

When the kind of online 'banter' experienced by PJ and Alfie stays among young players who have the emotional resilience to shake it off, it may seem harmless enough. However, as we saw from the Gamergate incident, gaming spaces can also breed hostile behaviour of a more sinister nature. The relative anonymity of gaming contributes to a sense of being permitted to speak and act without customary boundaries: 'I think you can really do whatever you feel [online] ... And in real life, you can be actually confronted about it and corrected ... Online it's not the same because you're just behind your screen, and you can just do whatever you want,' noted one seventeen-year-old interviewed in 2025.[22]

It is undeniable that many boys and men find a strong sense of enjoyment and community in gaming, but when this comes alongside repeated exposure to the normalised abuse of women, LGBTQI+ people and minorities, it can also lower their resistance to extremist messaging.[23] There is now plenty of evidence that some vulnerable boys are actively being recruited into violent ideologies online via gaming and gaming-adjacent platforms, including Discord.[24] Some horrific acts over the past few years, including the murders of fifty-one people in Christchurch, New Zealand, in 2021, where the killer shared his plans for the intended racist attack in a Discord server, before livestreaming it on Facebook, have raised awareness of the role played by these spaces in speeding up and intensifying the radicalisation process.[25]

Such cases, where online radicalisation fuels real-life violence, are at the very extreme end of internet dangers, but they have also drawn attention to the fact that live interactions between individuals in gaming-associated forums and in-game voice chat functions, despite some efforts by the tech platforms, are difficult to moderate due to the volume and ephemerality of the communications. Alfie alluded to this when we interviewed him: 'It's very, very easy to get in chats with loads of strangers. I think it's far too easy cos you can just invite anyone online. I think that's really bad from a safety point of view, especially the fact that you can just message someone on their account.' This is something which Amelia, as a parent of a teen boy, was not fully aware of at the time. We think it's vital that parents now are better informed about the grooming tactics used by some dangerous actors online.

Misogynists and other extremists can use in-game communication channels, in a context where the abuse of women and minorities is frequent, to lure boys to more private platforms such as Discord servers. These are private, invite-only forums, similar to WhatsApp groups or a mini social network, and largely unmoderated. There, more extreme ideologies can be propagated and nurtured.[26] These hateful communities use the most popular memes and language of gaming ('shit-posting', 'vibe-check', etc.) to encourage a sense of belonging among those who identify as members. Often, just as we saw in Calum's case, the boys most isolated in the real world are also most susceptible.

There are many examples of such spaces being used to plan and coordinate the online and real-world harassment of women – so-called 'hate raids'. These involve followers being prompted to inundate the pages or streams of prominent female creators and women-led organisations with invective and abuse. In one 2024 incident, approvingly dubbed 'Gamergate 2.0' by X proprietor Elon Musk, trolls bombarded a small video games consultancy accused of 'wokeifying' the latest in the Spider-Man game franchise.[27] The point of such activity is to claim gaming as a space exclusively for men, particularly white men, and warn off those seen as a threat to this territory-marking. Once again, we see women's attempts to take up space online ruthlessly sabotaged.

'How to Ascend'

As we've seen, manosphere subcultures prey on boys' everyday worries. Perfectly innocent searches for fitness, grooming and dating advice can quickly lead to 'self-improvement' content which pushes the narratives of masculinity as toughness, aggression and dominance over women. Alfie has been algorithmically exposed to this kind of content on Instagram and TikTok when searching up workout and sports videos:

> *The fitness stuff is everywhere and like 'bettering yourself' to be more of a man. I see a lot of that stuff and it's all about avoiding certain foods to boost your testosterone and that kind of thing ... eating raw meat and drinking raw eggs and stuff will make you more of a man. There might be a post where it's two columns and it'll be things that a boy does and then things that a man does, and it's eating certain foods that will lower your testosterone. It seems like it swerves from, you know, meal prepping and going to the gym to being more of a misogynistic 'you need to have the power!' kind of thing.*

The manosphere luminaries appear to be constantly dreaming up new ways to make young men feel inadequate. 'Looksmaxxing' is the latest increasingly noisy online movement to have migrated from some of the more extreme incel forums into mainstream spaces such as TikTok and Instagram.[28] This highly damaging trend stems from the idea that to increase their 'sexual market value' and 'ascend' (move up the sexual hierarchy), boys must go to extreme lengths to improve their looks. Looksmaxxing techniques, which include the use of growth hormones, cosmetic surgery, 'mewing' (facial exercises to improve the jawline) and 'bone smashing' (repeatedly hitting your own face with a hammer to build more prominent cheekbones), are promoted to boys on social media by influencers such as Clavicular, a Kick streamer. He has boasted of bone smashing and injecting steroids in pursuit of looksmaxxing, and even taking crystal meth as an appetite suppressant.[29] Needless to say, many of these influencers are monetising this harmful nonsense by peddling dubious supplements, courses and 'looksmaxxing kits' to their thousands of young followers.

Negative body image is an issue more often associated with teenage girls, but there is plenty of evidence that, faced with relentless exposure to unrealistic 'masculine' ideals online, boys are becoming more and more affected. One recent study found that 91 per cent of boys had seen body image content online, with 75 per cent seeing messaging about how to be more muscular. 24 per cent of boys agreed that social media makes them feel that they should change their looks. Those adolescent boys who were most exposed to problematic masculinity content online also appeared to be the most dissatisfied with their own body image, which is not surprising given the invariably demoralising and hectoring tone of the most followed voices of the manosphere.[30]

There is, of course, absolutely nothing wrong with boys seeking to adopt a fitness routine, or searching up advice on fashion and grooming, but some of the extreme regimes promoted online, from raw meat diets to over-strenuous exercise challenges to the use of steroids, promote an unrealistic ideal of the hyper-muscular male body. The incidence of eating disorders among boys has seen a huge increase over the last twenty years, with medical professionals identifying muscle dysmorphia, or 'bigorexia': the obsessive preoccupation with becoming more muscular.[31] Research from Movember found that men and boys who engage with online masculinity influencers are more likely to participate in a range of risky behaviours related to fitness, including working out while injured and taking performance-enhancing drugs and diet pills.[32]

We'll say it one more time for those at the back: the manosphere really does not have the best interests of boys and men at heart.

'They Want Us to Act like Porn Models'

At the beginning of this chapter, we noted that many parents and carers do not know a great deal about how their children spend time online. Sadly, we believe it is also true that there are some aspects of kids' digital lives some of us just *do not want* to know about. Parents have highlighted talking about pornography as the hardest conversation to have with their children.[33] I'm sure we can all relate to this. We are going to look at some ways to tackle tricky conversations later in the book. But, before we do, we will lay out a few reasons why this one is incredibly important to have with our kids – particularly boys, who are disproportionately consuming and affected by porn at an increasingly young age.

The Children's Commissioner, Rachel de Souza, has done amazing work in drawing attention to the harmful effects of early exposure to porn on boys and girls, and makes the point firmly that what children are seeing online these days bears no resemblance to the soft porn magazines and videos which parents may have encountered in their youth.

The vast majority of online porn depicts sexual aggression and violence towards women and teenage girls. The average age by which children see porn is now thirteen, and by the age of eighteen, 79 per cent of children have seen violent pornography.[34] Porn is now so ubiquitous and normalised across the internet and social media that it appears impossible for children to 'opt out', even with the recent changes to age verification requirements resulting from the Online Safety Act. PJ, for example, claims he saw explicit porn on his X (then Twitter) feed as a teenager from 2022, when its new owner Elon Musk drastically reduced moderation on the platform. Research confirms Twitter/X as the number one site where children (41 per cent of those surveyed) view pornography, with Instagram and Snapchat close behind.[35] If the UK government's plans for a social media ban achieve one thing, it must be to reduce children's exposure to porn. However, given their ingenuity, whatever restrictions are in place, it is probably realistic to assume that they will continue to encounter it earlier than we would wish.

Andrew Tate's appearances in playground chat have dwindled of late, but the same cannot be said for Bonnie Blue. If you haven't heard of her, Bonnie Blue is a porn actor famous for filming herself having sex with 1,000 men in a single day.[36] She has become a huge social media phenomenon across many platforms, from X, where some of her sexual exploits can be viewed uncensored, to TikTok, where she posts glamorous lifestyle content of her travels and pampering beauty treatments. As a sex worker, her pitch is explicitly to teenage boys: in 2024 and 2025, Blue embarked on a 'Bang Bus' tour of British universities where she encouraged ('barely legal') young men to come and have sex with her, for free, in return for featuring the content on her OnlyFans channel. She has also been described by Andrew Tate, with whom she has partnered on videos, as the 'ultimate endpoint of feminism'.[37]

Bonnie Blue's rise to fame is indicative not just of the normalisation of porn in the lives of children and young adults, but of the fact that the line is fast blurring between adult 'content creators' and more traditional social media influencers. Teacher Eoghan Cleary recently wrote about the popularity among young teenage girls at his school of the Bop House, a TikTok account posting fashion, beauty and lifestyle content from a group of OnlyFans models living in a 'porn production house' in Florida.

Unlike social media platforms, OnlyFans allows content creators to monetise their media directly. While some content is paywalled, requiring users to pay a monthly subscription, private pay-per-view transactions are also a feature of the platform. The creator base is largely women catering to a male audience, and its business model is frequently touted on social media as an easy way for young women to make vast sums of money. In Cleary's view, the glamorisation tactics of accounts such as the Bop House represent an attempt by the porn industry to appeal to younger and younger demographics.[38]

Of course, children should ideally not be accessing such age-inappropriate material as pornography *at all*. The fact that they do gives rise to a number of troubling consequences which we need to understand as the parents and carers of boys. Firstly, for some children explicit porn serves as their sex education. Pornography's often violent and degrading depiction of sex acts and unrealistically proportioned protagonists may be these kids' first introduction to what sex looks like. Secondly, this early exposure appears to be affecting boys' attitudes in ways that are very damaging for women and girls, and for their own mental and physical well-being.

Pornography usually presents women as objects to be humiliated, coerced and abused by men, solely in pursuit of their own pleasure. Often women are actually depicted as enjoying this treatment. The lines of consent in porn scenarios are often blurred and women's agency completely sidelined. As a result, young people who frequently consume pornography are more amenable to sexual 'scripts' (ideas of what is acceptable) that involve risky and violent sexual behaviours (coercion, choking, hitting, etc.). One girl interviewed for the Children's Commissioner's investigation commented: 'A lot of online pornography can be unrealistic and some of it is rape content, so young people may think this is okay and realistic. When in reality it is not acceptable, it teaches incorrect and disgusting behaviours.'[39] 50 per cent of police interviews in 2023 with children who reported sexual abuse by another child contained references to acts of sexual violence commonly found in porn.[40]

Porn use among young people is also associated over time with poorer body image and self-esteem, and an increase in sexist and objectified opinions of women. Most distressingly however, the viewing of violent porn has convincingly been linked to harmful changes in actual behaviour, with those who have viewed it nearly six times more likely to carry out acts of sexual aggression, even when other factors (such as alcohol use or having witnessed violence) are taken into account.[41] Researchers have also noticed a 'peer effect' of porn viewing where the negative attitudes and behaviour changes extend to the friends of those who have watched it, even if they haven't seen it themselves.[42] Thinking back to the 'pyramid of misogyny' (see p. 46), this suggests that 'porn chat' among teenagers may contribute to the normalisation of sexual aggression. Porn is becoming ubiquitous in mainstream content aimed at Gen Z audiences. Boys' ease of access to often extreme material, combined with the wider prevalence of misogyny on social media is creating a perfect storm, with girls and women bearing the brunt of harm.

The New Frontiers of Cyber Harm

Matteo recalled in Chapter Three how nude images of girls from school had sometimes been circulated digitally among the boys, and PJ recently confirmed that the same thing happened in his time at school. Boys have always been curious to see girls with their clothes off – that's nothing new – but sadly, technology has facilitated a huge rise in what is now called non-consensual image abuse. The impact on girls has been enormous. As well as having photos circulated (sometimes even taken in the first place) without their permission, girls are having to deal with frequent requests from boys to send sexual images and nudes and often feel pressured to do so. Boys, on the other hand, experience pressure to obtain such images, receiving points on the masculinity scale from their peers if they do. 'You're not man enough if you don't have any pictures,' as one Year Nine boy put it.[43]

Concerns around non-consensual image abuse have escalated further in response to some widely reported occurrences of British school boys sharing 'deepfakes' of girls known to them.[44] These images are easily created by children due to the horrifyingly easy availability of AI apps such as Nudify, which can create nude images in seconds from any girl or woman's uploaded image. One report found that nudifying apps had been advertised 10,000 times across Meta platforms.[45]

Non-consensual image abuse causes huge harm and mental distress, and it's instructive to look at the law's position at this point: some parents may be unaware, for example, that it is a criminal offence for *anybody* to possess or distribute nude or sexual images of children under eighteen. That means that a sixteen-year-old boy sharing images of a girl his own age, even if she consents, is committing a crime under the 2003 Sexual Offences Act. Following some highly publicised cases where the sharing was consensual between members of teenage couples, the College of Policing has published guidance to avoid overcriminalising children.[46] However, where the sharing is non-consensual and there is any coercion or malice involved, the Crown Prosecution Service is clear that there should be a full criminal investigation.

Such is the fear among girls of deepfake abuse that there is evidence some are actually decreasing their activity on social media for fear of their photographs being used in this way.[47]

The Online Safety Act has strengthened legislation on the sharing of intimate images to protect women and girls from the daily harassment caused by cyberflashing (colloquially, unsolicited 'dick pics'). Crucially, following a scandal in early 2026, when it was found that users were prompting X's native AI chatbot, Grok, to undress pictures of women and children, the new laws on non-consensual image abuse make no distinction between real images and deepfakes, closing a previously overlooked loophole.[48] However, it's hard for legislation such as the Online Safety Act to keep pace with the speed of new tech, and in the AI age, new challenges are already emerging. Some men are already reporting that they are becoming addicted to extreme and surreal AI porn, which can be easily generated and distributed online.[49]

With young people's mental health declining, loneliness on the rise and access to talking therapies often restricted to those who can pay for it, many teenagers are turning to AI chatbots such as Grok or ChatGPT for advice and support. But even there, the guardrails may not yet be in place to allow for the safe and healthy use of this new technology. The parents of Adam Raine, who committed suicide at the age of sixteen, filed a lawsuit against Open AI in August 2025, maintaining that the company prioritised engagement over safety in developing the GPT-4o app and that it encouraged their son's suicidal impulses.

One paediatrician interviewed in 2025 observed, 'It's a very new technology ... It's ever-changing and there's not really best practices for youth yet. So, I think there are more opportunities now for risks because we're still kind of guinea pigs in the whole process.'[50] Once again, our kids are acting as 'guinea pigs' in an experiment prompted by novel technology which may have dangerous unintended consequences.

Criminals are also dreaming up new ways to exploit boys' sexual curiosity. In 2024, US teenager Evan Boettler committed suicide after falling victim to a scammer on Snapchat who had persuaded him they were a teenage girl. After asking Evan to share nude pictures, the scammer then began ruthlessly blackmailing him, demanding money to prevent them releasing the images publicly. The BBC uncovered a whole criminal network of such swindlers in Lagos, Nigeria. When asked why they targeted boys, one responded: 'Because their sex drive is so high, and young boys are scared of their pictures being released to their class groups, their parents and their friends.'[51]

Even more serious are the terrifying acts of sextortion and incitement to self-harm, and even suicide, carried out by members of online 'satanist' groups such as 764 and the various 'Com' networks. Those members include British teenager Cameron Finnigan, who was jailed for six years in 2025 for encouraging suicide and possessing indecent images of children.[52] Another horrific instance is the infamous South Korean chatroom network, the Nth Room, where dozens of women and girls were sexually exploited between 2018 and 2020.[53]

The online world our boys are living in is vast, complicated and dangerous, but it can also be enriching. Most of the time when they are on their smartphones, we are quite sure that your sons will be happily watching mountain biking videos on Instagram or goal compilations of their favourite footballers on YouTube. We've drawn your attention to some of the more dangerous content that boys are exposed to because evidence shows it is having a damaging impact on the way they think about, and treat, women and girls. This is emphatically not the fault of boys themselves.

As we've asserted before, certain individuals see boys and young men's insecurities as a way to get rich, while they simultaneously promote a sick ideology which drives a wedge between men and women and harms all genders. This has to change, and we believe we can all work together to make that happen.

Before we begin to explore how we do that, let's go back to Calum, whose loneliness during Covid drove him into the slimy embrace of the manosphere. We asked him, what brought him out of it? How did he manage to escape? His answers were very insightful and echoed much of what we know from our own work about how and why people are able to change their minds and divert from a dangerous ideology. It turns out that open communication and empathetic conversations were the most important factors driving Calum's reappraisal of the ideology that had captured him. Once lockdown was over and he found himself back in school as a sixth-former, Calum started interacting more with other students, including girls, Muslim kids and LGBTQI+ people – just making general small talk at lunch and hanging out. He began comparing the easy relations he had with diverse individuals at school with the demonising rhetoric coming from those he followed online. Calum's personal experiences began to contradict these narratives. If feminists and Muslims were evil, for example, why were people who identified as such sympathetic and friendly to him? The arguments fell apart on contact with the reality of one-to-one communication. In a polarised world where it sometimes feels as though people are screaming at one another across an ever-increasing divide, it's time to talk, and listen.

PART THREE
REMEDIES

Chapter 7

How to Talk so Boys Will Listen

The clichéd teenage boy, a familiar staple from films, sitcoms and soaps, is a gawky, often hygiene-challenged male who lurks in his bedroom surrounded by junk food packaging and communicates via the odd grunt. While teenage girls busily invent new slang and speech forms to the extent that experts have called them 'linguistic innovators', we mostly take it for granted that boys will become more taciturn as they enter adolescence.[1]

During the teenage years, both boys and girls begin to distance themselves from the rest of the family as their desire for privacy increases and they start to grow into their own distinct personality traits. In turn, they tend to place much more weight on being accepted and respected by their peers, whether in online spaces or in real life.[2] This differentiation is a normal part of child development – nothing new there. What it does not signal, however much their behaviour may suggest otherwise, is a wish to renounce the support and safety of the parental relationship. We think it's important not to draw the conclusion that a boy's withdrawal is a cue to leave him to his own devices (pun intended). There aren't any shortcuts here: clear, loving and, above all, frequent communication with boys, while respecting their growing independence, is the only way to monitor their overall emotional health.

If there is one thing we know from our work at Shout Out UK, it's that the key to inoculating and freeing young people from the traps of ideological extremism is open, authentic and non-judgemental conversation. For our podcast *Media Minded*, Matteo has interviewed many people who have escaped from the grasp of toxic ideologies and conspiracy theories, including cult members and anti-vaxxers. Just like Calum in the previous chapter, most of them confirmed that a conversation with an empathetic listener was usually the trigger that caused them to question their beliefs and open their minds to other possibilities.

Understanding Boys' Emotional Lives

Empathy – the ability to see and feel things from others' perspectives – does not feature among the stereotypically male qualities of the 'man box'. Psychologists have found that in early childhood boys and girls show similar levels of empathy and the desire to care for others, but as children enter adolescence, boys begin to lag behind.[3] As boys are initiated at school into a peer culture which prizes confidence, dominance, heterosexuality and physical prowess, they quickly learn that talking about their feelings is taboo. Groups of boys can be fiercely competitive and exclusionary, largely reflecting the adult norms of masculinity they see around them. Those who don't conform are frequently mocked and sometimes bullied.[4] For too many boys, this jostling for masculine status at school heralds the start of a lifetime's habit of 'masking' their real emotional life.

Studies have shown that as boys mature into men, their faces become less emotionally expressive. The reverse is true for women.[5] Caring itself is gendered – with girls praised for expressing tenderness and empathy, and boys often penalised for the same by their peers and even adults. In a homophobic, patriarchal culture, these feelings are classed as 'gay' or 'girly' – some of the worst insults which boys can level at each other.

Despite a social environment where they are often discouraged from expressing their feelings and showing care for others, most boys, like most humans, are naturally empathetic and inclined to seek out close bonds with others. But even in male friendships based on genuine mutual affection, a model of communication based on 'banter' may sometimes make it more difficult to start conversations about the everyday worries and challenges that men face, for fear that friends may not be receptive to chat taking a more serious turn.

Opportunities for real-life meet-ups are less common now than they used to be for teenagers, with schoolwork often taking priority over hanging out with friends. A 2025 survey found that 72 per cent of teenage boys said they had only one person in their lives who knows them 'really well'.[6] Many boys are experiencing loneliness and craving deep and fulfilling connections with family, friends and partners who will listen to their perspectives and sympathise. Too often, though, the emotional skills which we all need to maintain positive relationships are depicted in the culture around us as purely the business of women and girls. This can mean that boys and young men struggle to ask for the emotional support they need. Alternatively, they may rely entirely on female friends and relatives to cater to their emotional needs, while often being able to offer little in the way of care in return.

The influencers of the manosphere pull off a very clever trick: while maintaining that radical 'independence' is a core pillar of masculinity, they simultaneously prey on boys who are seeking the emotional validation and feeling of belonging which they may struggle to find in the real world. However, it's been shown that men who most value the hyper-masculine qualities these influencers promote, including 'restrictive emotionality', appear to show higher levels of sexism and hostility towards women.[7]

Conversely, having close emotional bonds with others is one of the most effective protective factors against extremism. In trusting relationships, views can be aired, argued through and challenged. Boys who have people close to them who they can confide in, and who give them alternative viewpoints, are less likely to fall victim to the influence of grievance narratives which blame others for their life problems.[8] It seems that modelling to boys how to healthily express and regulate their emotions may actively disrupt those narratives which hold women responsible for men's loneliness and inability to connect with others.

As parents, we need to teach and value emotional literacy in boys to the same extent as we do in girls. Despite what some in the manosphere might claim, this is not about 'feminising' them – just allowing them greater emotional freedom. We need to permit boys, from babyhood onwards, to express normal feelings such as sadness or pain and avoid language that stigmatises them for doing so, such as 'Man up!' or 'Don't be such a girl!'

Dads and male carers, in particular, are well placed to model to boys a different kind of masculinity which prizes kindness and empathy over dominance and repression.[9] If we can show boys that caring for others, expressing vulnerability and asking for help with challenges are not actions confined to one gender, then they will be more likely to share their anxieties with us, and less likely to seek answers from strangers online.

We can also demonstrate to them how their anger (the only emotion that is more acceptable for men than for women) can be healthily contained and redirected (for example into positive pastimes, or physical exercise), rather than finding an outlet in resentment, hostility or even violence.

How to Listen So Boys Will Talk

The online manosphere capitalises on the trope of male 'stoicism' to persuade boys that they need to tackle their problems alone, and that they are weak and pathetic if they can't.[10] So how do we break down this shaming narrative and offer an alternative?

In our work at Shout Out UK we emphasise the effectiveness of empathetic listening to help young people develop the emotional resilience to be able to hear opposing viewpoints in conversation without flying off the handle. The reality is that no one ever changed their mind because they were forced into doing so, or told they were stupid for believing something in the first place. In fact, this can make people double down on their professed beliefs, *particularly* teenagers, who may be actively looking for opportunities to rebel against or shock their parents.

If our goal is to protect boys from extremist or isolating viewpoints, the most powerful advantage is a parent or carer who is a safe space, rather than a judge. Learning how to listen so boys will feel confident enough to talk is the first step in building an atmosphere of mutual emotional trust and security.

So, what might this look like in practice when responding to boys repeating some of the biased or sexist messages they have learned from the manosphere? The table below compares the fear-based 'reactive' listening style which we may default to as anxious parents, with the more constructive tools of empathetic listening.

Reactive Listening	Empathetic Listening
Interrupting a boy, or jumping in with a shocked response like 'Where did you hear that nonsense?' or an angry counter-argument.	Allowing the boy to speak freely first, and actively listening. Avoiding shouting or shaming. This may trigger a defensive reaction, or even rebellion.
Criticising them for believing a trope or stereotype.	Investigating *why* the message resonated with them. Asking open-ended questions: 'Why does that idea appeal to you?' or 'How does this relate to your experiences?'
Shutting down the conversation (censorship).	Encouraging open debate and discussion. Allowing them to finish their thought completely before you respond. This proves you aren't 'censoring' them, neutralising the manosphere narrative that men are being 'silenced'.
Can result in boys doubling down on their views.	Builds emotional resilience and trust.

The Critical Thinking Toolkit

It's our belief that instilling emotional intelligence and resilience in boys *and* girls, and maintaining a home environment where open and non-judgemental discussion is the default, are essential to raising young people who are resistant to extreme ideologies. We know that our kids are exposed to a torrent of potentially confusing and harmful messages online. So before they start to negotiate these digital spaces alone, we must also proactively equip them with specific media literacy skills.

As we write this book, the daily news headlines present a series of new and constantly evolving scenarios relating to children and tech. A quick glance online throws up new reports on the dangers of teens using ChatGPT for counselling advice, extremists recruiting on Roblox, and the impact of short-form video on children's brain development, among many others. It's unrealistic to think that we can completely protect teenagers from every technological development that might affect their well-being – the pace of change is simply too rapid. What we can do is teach them how to respond healthily to what they find online.

Critical thinking refers to the process of scrutinising and thinking analytically about the information we encounter in our daily lives. When we think critically, we approach events, stories, social media posts or other texts with a mindset trained to establish their credibility, accuracy and potential to cause harm. Once learned, these skills stay with us for the rest of our lives, helping us to make better informed decisions and avoid mistakes and harm. They are vital to helping boys resist misogynistic narratives.

The critical thinking toolkit that we teach in schools in our work at Shout Out UK is made up of media and digital literacy skills which help young people distinguish harmful from harmless, and real from fake, online.

These are the skills that will enable boys to see past the dubious claims, stereotypes, misleading news stories and toxic social media content they see on a daily basis. Online misogyny spreads due to misinformation and disinformation about women and gender, so it's important to develop the ability to recognise it, both on and offline, even when it may initially appear innocuous.

Media Literacy[II]	**Digital Literacy**
The ability to access and navigate different platforms and news sources; understanding your rights as an internet user.	Proficiency in the use of hardware and software and managing your personal data.
The ability to decode how media messages are constructed, including the role of algorithms and AI.	Algorithmic literacy: understanding how search engines and social feeds filter the information you see.
The ability to critically assess and verify content, and identify mis- and disinformation.	The ability to assess the security of digital platforms and data sources.
The ability to use media to engage in open debate and to counter hate speech or radicalisation.	The understanding that digital actions may have real-world and societal impact.
The awareness of one's own biases and echo chambers.	The ability to maintain privacy and online safety.
The ability to produce your own media messages which respect others' rights and avoid harm.	The ability to use digital tools and software to help with practical tasks and for self-expression.

A few years ago, Matteo interviewed William Brustein, a leading expert on antisemitism.[12] He introduced us to the idea of the 'nugget of truth' that often lies at the heart of conspiracy theories. This is the idea that a hateful belief used to justify the persecution of a group may have metastasised from a tiny nugget of truth. For example: in the case of antisemitism, Jewish people were historically denied access to many professions, but were permitted to work as money-lenders. This fact has systematically been exaggerated and embroidered on over the years to stigmatise them as mercenary and miserly.[13]

In the case of misogyny, manosphere influencers can exploit a nugget of truth, such as the stats in a single survey of dating app users which they claim prove the 80/20 rule, to draw boys into conspiracy theories which exploit their insecurities.[14] If you feel a boy has been hoodwinked into a harmful belief, it will often be because this 'nugget' has triggered a valid anxiety (in this case, that girls may not find him attractive). So make sure you ask questions about *why* a particular narrative might have resonated with him in the first place.

As we have noted elsewhere, preventing misogynistic behaviours in our boys has to start with ourselves. As parents and carers, we first need to critically assess our own behaviours by thinking about the gender biases that may influence our own thinking. Of course, we all have biases and preferences – and that's entirely normal. More often than not, these are totally harmless and don't impact others. For example, avoiding certain kinds of foods because we don't like them, or choosing a certain product because we prefer the brand.

'Confirmation bias' is the phenomenon of being more likely to credit information that backs up our existing preferences. For example, Matteo pays much more attention to health information that highlights the benefits of drinking red wine and eating chocolate than to articles that lead on the negative effects of these treats on cholesterol levels! Most of our biases are not harmful, because they don't have any impact on other people or *their* choices. But when biases have a negative effect on others, they become a problem – especially if based on something a person can't help, like their race, sexuality or gender.

To explore and manage your own biases concerning gender, we recommend stopping to ask yourself a few questions before acting or making a comment, and teaching children to do likewise, for example:

- Could this action be considered sexist?
- Does this action or comment play into stereotypes about women, or feed stereotypical narratives that I know to be harmful?
- What is the intention of my comment, and what unintended impact might my comment have?
- Where did I hear this comment or idea before it occurred to me to repeat it?

If you're not 100 per cent sure whether the behaviour or content you're seeing could be considered misogynistic, you could and should ask yourself:

- Does this content play into stereotypes about women, or feed harmful narratives?
- What was the reaction of the other people who witnessed it (in the comments section, for example, if online)?
- What was the intention of the speaker or poster? What was their tone, or goal?

- What was the impact on the people who witnessed it?
- Has there been a pattern of misogynistic comments from the same source or person in the past?

Thinking through the answers to these questions and engaging critically with the behaviour we see around us and online helps us to identify misogyny as we encounter it and develop empathy for its victims. By teaching boys to do the same, we can actively reduce the opportunity for the evangelists of misogyny to spread their hate.

Prebunking: How to Challenge Misogyny Before It Tales Hold

Taking action early and having pre-emptive discussions with your boys on the topics we've discussed in this book will create a home environment where misogyny and online abuse is not normalised or considered okay. These techniques are known as 'prebunking' – a way to prevent the negative impact of harmful content by pre-empting and countering its messaging in advance.

As we've seen, online misogyny shows up in diverse ways, often appearing in boys' feeds in the guise of softer content such as fitness advice, so it's crucial to make sure the critical skills we teach them take these factors into account. Boys need to learn, first of all, how to establish the informational integrity of online content:

- Is the poster or source of information reliable and qualified to inform on this topic?

- Are their claims, stories, statistics or arguments factually correct, or are they based on opinion or personal experience?
- If there are videos or images, is there a possibility these visuals have been AI-generated or edited; or is it possible they are deepfakes?

Once they have established if this information is based in fact or opinion, we should encourage boys to engage critically regarding the poster's *reasons* for sharing the content, allowing them to determine for themselves whether any potential harm is intended. Watching the content with them and asking the following questions might be helpful here:

- Could the information shared be harmful to a particular audience, in this case, women and girls?
- Does this person, account or source of information frequently post about sex or gender?
- Does it appear the person is purposefully trying to convince others, particularly boys and young men, of their claims or beliefs?
- How does this content make me feel? Does it appear intended to provoke a strong emotional response, like anger, fear or even laughter?

If they do come across a harmful or misogynistic piece of content, boys can then use the answers to those questions to consider:

- blocking the user,
- avoiding interacting with the source of the content,

- making trusted adults around them aware of what they have seen.

FACTS

Here is a snappy media literacy mnemonic to teach your kids from as soon as they venture online unaccompanied:

F: Find the claim or information you want to check.
A: Analyse the source and look for credibility.
C: Cross-check the information with many reliable sources.
T: Take note of any biases or misleading elements.
S: Seek expert opinions or verified sources to validate the information.

Debunking: How to Stop Misogyny in Its Tracks

We've seen how pervasive and influential the online manosphere is, so even when you think you've instilled in kids the practices of critical thinking and prebunking, they can still easily fall prey to the most insidious and commonplace sexist narratives, such as the 80/20 rule, or that girls prefer men who treat them badly. If you have concerns that a boy is repeating manosphere talking points approvingly, the best way to tackle it is to start a judgement-free conversation about it.

In recent years, some online voices have promoted an aggressive 'call-out culture', where we are encouraged to immediately name and shame those who express views we deem unacceptable or disagree with.[15] Like many experts we find these tactics to be completely counter-productive. In fact, rather than neutralising harmful views, they may actually further radicalise those at risk.[16]

We favour a contrasting approach called 'calling in', which emphasises 'helping a person learn rather than trying to change them'.[17] Instead of trying to replace someone's beliefs with your own, 'calling in' means encouraging them to consider new information or different perspectives, but it can only be done when that person feels that their own viewpoint has first been listened to respectfully.

Rising to the bait when a boy makes a provocative comment, or responding with panic, risks potentially escalating a conversation into a lecture, or worse, a row. As an alternative, we think it's worth taking a deep breath and doing something communication experts call 'adding meaning to the pool' of the conversation.[18] This means sharing additional information which the boy may not have considered, offering your own or many other viewpoints in a calm and considered way, for example: 'I have come across the belief that 80 per cent of women are only attracted to 20 per cent of men, but in my personal experience, the maths doesn't stack up,' or, 'I have definitely heard it said that women often make false allegations of sexual assault, but I also read a piece which offered strong evidence that the real incidence of this was actually very low. Why don't I send you the link so you can take a look and see what you think?'

To do this with authority, it might be worth arming yourself in advance with some data (perhaps from Chapters Two and Three of this book) which directly contradict the manosphere's most repeated falsehoods.

The most direct debunking approach is to ask the boy to show you the content on their phone, watch it together and then tailor the questions you ask to the exact narrative shown in the content. This will come much more naturally if you habitually show interest in what he is looking at online – sharing videos and memes, say, which you have enjoyed or think he might like. When chatting about digital consumption is normalised in families, kids are more likely to respond positively and with introspection to your questions and observations. And if you've viewed the content yourself, you will be better placed to introduce the possibility of doubt, without needing to blame the boy for expressing a specific point of view.

Another tactic is to offer information which suggests to the individual expressing extreme adherence to a particular ideology that they might be being manipulated or conned.[19] For teenagers who want to feel they are growing in agency, this can be an effective prompt for them to start to question some of the narratives they have been repeating. Again, this can be done in a way that observes rather than scolds: 'Wow, that guy's videos certainly get you riled up. I guess he makes more money from the algorithm that way.' By doing this, you are usefully highlighting the need to examine the motives of those who distribute content designed to be highly emotive – a vital twenty-first-century life skill for young adults.

Remember: listening to your son's viewpoint does not mean endorsing it, and it's okay to express disapproval if you feel a line has been crossed. The most persuasive way to do this is always to condemn the belief, or those who originate it, rather than the boy himself. As we've shown, boys are the first victims of online misogynists. We need to be showing them a better way to be men, rather than castigating them for consuming content which finds its way to them even if they don't seek it out.

Another way we've found effective in discussing online content with boys, while maintaining an empathetic approach, is to appeal to their better natures by calling them in from a position of shared values. The adults in the family should establish firmly that while all viewpoints are listened to and engaged with, certain beliefs, such as that everyone should be respected regardless of their race or gender, are fundamental to their moral world view.

A Step-by-Step Guide to Talking to Boys About the Manosphere

Once you feel ready to open a difficult conversation with a boy, first find the right place to broach it with them. This will vary from family to family: some boys will be more likely to open up on a walk or car drive, for example, as a side-by-side interaction can feel less challenging or confrontational than face to face. Once you've found a safe and comfortable environment for this discussion, you can engage calmly.

- Ask the boy where he developed these opinions and what convinced him that the misogynistic claim was true.
- Listen carefully to his views and show that you are willing to hear what he thinks before attempting to debunk his claim. You can show you are listening by saying things like, 'Mmm, go on,' and, 'Okay I see,' but don't interrupt him.
- When it seems appropriate in the conversation, you can introduce some open-ended questions to make him

think a bit more deeply about the content he has seen online. These might include:

- 'What do you think the intention was behind that video? Why was the content posted? What are the motivations of the person who posted it?'
- 'Do any of the statements seem exaggerated, or sweeping generalisations (for example, "all women are like that")? How do you think that content would make a girl or woman feel?'
- 'It seems like this content made you feel angry – why is that?'

- You may also consider using counter-messaging techniques: using a story that counters the misogynistic view or claim to demonstrate that it may be inaccurate or maliciously intended. It might be helpful here to search for the 'nugget of truth' at the heart of the belief and offer further context and examples which restore a fuller picture. Remember too that, for Calum, counter-messaging that he encountered in the real world, such as girls at school being friendly and supportive of him, was one of the key elements that snapped him out of his misogynist views. The stories you use will obviously be very personal depending on the family circumstances, but some effective and positive counter-messages might be:
  - Referring to the boy's relationships with women and girls they know, such as teachers, friends or even celebrities they admire: 'Your cousin Libby is studying to be a doctor. How do you think she would feel about the idea that women are less intelligent than men?'

– Relating the comment or opinion to your own family: 'How would you feel if I/your mum/your sister/your granny was talked about/treated like that?'

Try to keep your tone light, friendly and supportive, so the boy doesn't feel they are being criticised or punished. As we've seen the 'red pill' lore explicitly primes boys for being challenged on their views by adults, teaching them to beware being brainwashed by mainstream society, so the aim is to stimulate the boy's own critical thinking, rather than imposing your own viewpoint.

The Conversations

Every boy, family and parental relationship is different and, while some of the issues we've discussed can be pre-empted with children, others will arise naturally in conversation and need to be addressed in the moment. We are sharing a set of common scenarios you might encounter below. However, rather than offering a set of scripts to follow, we consider it more important to leave you with some ideas of how the techniques we've outlined can be adapted to varying circumstances. Our blended SOUK approach to talking to boys about the harmful beliefs they may encounter online combines:

- listening without judgement,
- media literacy prebunking and debunking tools,
- critical thinking,
- 'calling in' rather than criticising.

Above all, we believe in developing the healthy emotional expression and empathy that will strengthen boys' resistance to an ideology which offers an easy scapegoat for the real challenges they face.

Scenario One: Manosphere Narratives

Boy citing a manosphere trope such as the 'gold digger' narrative that women are only interested in men who have a lot of money.

The Trap (what to avoid)

Reacting with panic or alarm or trying to shut down the conversation: 'That's just ridiculous. I don't care where you've heard that, I don't want you repeating it again.'

The SOUK Approach (Debunking)

Step 1: Listen without judgement. Show you are willing to hear him out first.

> *Parent: 'Mmm, okay. Go on.'*

Step 2: Add meaning to the pool. Offer a different viewpoint calmly, without invalidating him.

> *Parent: 'That belief has been around for ages. In my opinion, it's based on a sexist stereotype that's unfair.'*

Step 3: Question the source's motive. Trigger introspection about the influencer.

> *Parent: 'Why do you think that influencer is posting that? Do you think being controversial helps him get more views or make money from the algorithm?'*

Step 4: Personalise it (counter-messaging). Use a trusted female figure as a reference.

Parent: 'It's lucky your mum doesn't think that way isn't it, or she'd never have married a poor teacher like me.'

Scenario Two: Pre-emptive Conversation about Porn

You want to prepare your child for the inevitable algorithmic push of sexually explicit content before he encounters it.

The Trap (what to avoid)

Treating the subject as taboo or 'dirty', or waiting until you find something on his phone to react angrily.

The SOUK Approach (Prebunking)

Step 1: Show you understand the digital reality that this content will find him without him looking for it.

Parent: 'You know, social media feeds are designed to keep you scrolling, and sometimes they push content that isn't suitable for kids, including adults having sex, just to get engagement.'

Step 2: Critical thinking questions. Teach him to question the intent of the content.

Parent: 'If you see anything like that, I want you to ask yourself a few questions. "Why am I being shown this content? Is it making me feel shocked or excited just to keep me watching?"'

Step 3: Shared values. Anchor the conversation in your family's moral world view regarding respect (particularly for women and girls).

Parent: 'In our family, we believe sexual relationships are based on mutual respect and enjoyment. Does that video show respect to the women involved, or is it treating them like objects?'

Scenario Three: Sexist Shaming or Stereotyping

The boy makes a comment like 'Girls can't drive' or 'Women are too emotional to be leaders.'

The Trap (What to avoid)

Immediately 'calling him out' or labelling him sexist. This risks him becoming defensive and doubling down.

The SOUK Approach (Calling In)

Step 1: Call in/ask for evidence. Encourage him to check the source or consider new information.

Parent: 'That's a very bold claim. Where did you hear that idea before it occurred to you to repeat it?'

Step 2: Check for generalisation. Ask if the statement might be a sweeping generalisation.

Parent: 'Do you think all women are like that, or is that just a stereotype you saw in a meme?'

Step 3: Empathy check. Ask him to consider the impact of the words on others.

Parent: 'How do you think hearing that would make your sister or your friend Sarah feel?'

Parent: 'Does that comment play into bigger ideas about women and girls that might actually be harmful?'

Scenario Four: Misinformation

You suspect he is consuming manosphere content designed to manipulate or provoke extreme views.

The Trap (what to avoid)

Banning the device or lecturing him on 'fake news'.

The SOUK Approach (Critical Thinking Toolkit)

Step 1: Assess credibility. Teach him to check the source using **FACTS** (see p. 174).

Parent: 'Hmm, let's take a look together. That video seems pretty intense. Is the person posting it actually qualified to talk about this, or is it just their opinion?'

Step 2: Check for manipulation. Look for AI or deepfakes.

Parent: 'The visuals look rather unrealistic. Do you think there is a possibility that the image has been AI-generated or edited to make us react?'

Step 3: Actionable steps. Remind him he has autonomy.

Parent: 'If an account makes you feel angry or bad about yourself, remember you can block the user or just stop interacting with them. You don't have to let them into your feed.'

Scenario Five: Being Turned Down by a Girl

He has been rejected by a girl he is interested in romantically and feels angry or humiliated.

The Trap (what to avoid)

Telling him to toughen up or dismissing his feelings with 'there are plenty more fish in the sea'.

The SOUK Approach (Emotional Literacy)

Step 1: Acknowledge the emotion. Allow him to express sadness or pain freely.

> *Parent: 'I can see you're extremely upset. It's completely normal to feel sad or even angry when things don't go the way we want in life.'*

Step 2: Redirect, don't repress. Help him manage the anger healthily.

> *Parent: 'It's okay to be angry, but instead of staying at home and brooding, why not burn it off by coming on a run with me?'*

Step 3: Inoculate against grievance. Prevent him from sliding into blame-based narratives.

> *Parent: 'I know it's hard right now, but one rejection doesn't mean there is something wrong with you, or that 'women' are the problem. She just wasn't the right one for you.'*

Upstanding: Challenging Misogyny

Once you are confident that boys have mastered the techniques of prebunking and debunking misogynist content themselves, you may feel they are ready to be introduced to the idea of 'upstanding'. Upstanding means speaking out against harmful content or behaviour (in our case misogyny) as it is happening, to prevent it from escalating or happening again. This can be done by highlighting or condemning the behaviour, and by supporting the intended target.[20] Showing the perpetrator that you've observed an act of hate take place is an important first step in minimising the likelihood of its recurrence, but there is a fine line to walk here. It need not necessarily mean loudly announcing what has happened, and most boys, even the most well intentioned, would likely be reluctant to do this in any case. But it could take the form of boys reporting an online user, approaching the person who expressed a misogynistic belief one to one to let them know their behaviour was not okay, or just calmly reporting what they have seen to a trusted adult.

Other effective ways to upstand can include:

- Interrupting comments or behaviours *as they are occurring*:
  - Perhaps asking a question to distract the person who is making a harmful comment.
  - Suggesting their comment or behaviour is inappropriate, and offering a more balanced viewpoint.
  - Asking the abuser directly to stop if you see a girl or woman being targeted online (for example, in gaming lobbies).

- Not every boy will have the confidence to intervene directly, but there also are other, less direct, ways to upstand which include:
  - Taking a note of events or comments to report later to a trusted adult.
  - Speaking directly to the girl or woman targeted to let them know you saw what happened.
  - Supporting the victim to make a complaint to the relevant platform and corroborating their account of the abuse or harassment.
- It's important to make sure boys understand there is a right and wrong way to upstand:
  - Two wrongs don't make a right. Never use aggression or violence against the person who has behaved, or been accused of behaving, in a misogynist way.
  - Look after your own safety first and make sure you are in a safe position to intervene.
  - If you choose to challenge the behaviour of someone who has behaved harmfully, be sure to challenge respectfully.

Once your boys feel empowered to upstand, both online and in the real world, they will form part of a first-line defence against misogyny. To paraphrase the famous quote, misogyny thrives when good men and boys do nothing.

When to Seek Professional Help

As we have said throughout the book, very few boys are likely to be radicalised by the manosphere to the extent that they will plan or carry out real-world violence such as the murder so chillingly depicted in *Adolescence*. However, if you come across any evidence that boys are making threats of violence online, or threatening or planning violent acts, you *must* notify the police immediately with the details you have. The UK government's Prevent strategy can also help if you're concerned that a boy is particularly vulnerable to extreme beliefs, and you can find relevant resources to guide you through this at the back of this book.

Additionally, it is worth bearing in mind that experts are learning that poor mental health may play a role in susceptibility to extreme beliefs and behaviour.[21] The data shows us that boys' mental health has taken a nosedive since the pandemic years, so it's important to look out for signs of depression, anxiety, eating disorders and other forms of mental illness in boys, which may not be obvious, particularly given the emphasis placed in the manosphere – and our wider culture – on men not showing any feelings or weakness.

Though none of the below behaviours is necessarily a cause for concern in isolation, it is worth being aware of the NHS's checklist of indicators for mental distress in children:

- Changes in appearance, such as dramatic weight loss or gain.
- Changes in mood or demeanour.
- Talking much more, or much less, than usual.

- Irritability.
- Becoming withdrawn.
- Becoming forgetful.
- Obsessive working out.
- Restrictive diets.
- Falling behind with schoolwork or other tasks.
- Avoiding social situations, even school.

If you are concerned about a boy, the first step should always be to make an appointment for them at your family GP, or encourage them to do so for themselves if they are a young adult.[22] There are more resources for supporting boys' mental health in the Resources section at the back of the book.

To ensure online misogyny ends with their generation, it's vital that we do all we can to help our boys grow up to be responsible and caring online citizens. Cultivating a family environment where kids can share opinions and problems without fearing that they will be shamed or punished is a crucial first step in that process. Bolstering your own and your family's media literacy skills with some of the techniques we've outlined will further strengthen boys' resilience to false narratives and online hate.

We hope this chapter has left you with increased confidence to talk to boys about what can be difficult, embarrassing and even upsetting topics. Remember, the most fruitful conversations are those based on honesty, mutual respect and connection. We can't promise that you won't ever lose it and express your own disgust or anger at something a boy has said. But hopefully, grounding your communication using some of these tools will prove useful. We look forward to hearing how you get on!

Chapter 8

Parenting 3.0

If you have bought this book because you are feeling concerned, guilty, confused or ill-equipped to handle the complex realities of the digital lives of the boys in your life, we just want to tell you one thing: we can relate. As parents from two different generations, we have both experienced all of those feelings around kids and tech.

Parenting has changed a great deal over the last fifty years. The social, political and economic changes which have transformed our world have also stimulated a shift in how we parent and, in turn, how successful parenting is perceived by society at large. We may think of family life as something restricted to hearth and home, our own little private world once we close the front door, but even our closest interpersonal relationships play out against the backdrop of a wider context. Since the middle of the last century, the movement for equal rights, the growth of consumer capitalism, women's mass entry into the labour market, and the rapid rise of digital technologies have all played a part in changing family dynamics and what is considered 'good parenting'.

Over this period, the traditional Victorian view of parenting – which dictated rules from above to children who should preferably be seen and not heard, and packed off to either work or boarding school (depending on social class) as soon as possible – has been transformed. As the post-war social contract improved living conditions, parents became freer to embrace different 'parenting philosophies' according to their values; for most, this led to a more egalitarian mode of family life.

Modern child and developmental psychologists have historically mapped parenting styles on an axis of warmth and control, the four main ones being:

- permissive or indulgent: high warmth, low control;
- neglectful: low warmth, low control;
- authoritarian: high control, low warmth; and
- authoritative: high warmth, high control,

with most experts considering the latter the most beneficial for children's well-being.[1]

Authoritative parenting, unlike the authoritarian 'top-down' model we may recognise from earlier times, relies on a trusting parental relationship. Parents impose rules on their kids, but they explain why (in an age-appropriate way), hoping that by doing so, children will be inspired to comply in their own best interests. Experts think that this equips kids better for decision-making as teens and adults, getting them used to the idea of weighing up the short- and long-term benefits and disadvantages of any particular action – a vital life skill.[2]

The authoritative model has inspired most of the recent advice offered to parents, whether from popular parenting websites and blogs or more official state-backed sources, such as the NHS, which recommends 'positive parenting': building close bonds with children, explaining the reasoning behind the rules that protect them, and rewarding good behaviour, rather than relying on punishment.[3] The Local Government Association website's stance is typical: 'Authoritative parenting predicts the best outcomes across wellbeing, health, and educational attainment.'[4]

This resonates with both of us: setting firm boundaries for children's behaviour within a warm and loving family environment is where we have both tried to ground our parenting practice, as we are sure most readers have too.

However, many parents now feel that the advance of digital technologies into almost every aspect of our lives has had an impact on their ability to practise the authoritative style.[5] As children's use of the internet has grown, so has its intrusion into family life, generating an increasingly noisy global conversation about its effects on child development and learning, how it should be monitored at home, and the risks vs harms of this digital engagement.

Authoritative parenting requires parents to be, well, authoritative: trusting their instincts and close knowledge of their individual child to know how to act in their best interests and develop their own ability to do the same. But there is no clear roadmap yet for parents to help us work out how to do this in the digital world. Our own older relatives, having not faced it themselves, certainly can't help us out as they might with some other parenting dilemmas. Parents take well-known and time-honoured steps to prepare their younger children for 'stranger danger' or safely crossing the road, but what is the equivalent process for teaching our kids how to maximise the positive possibilities of the internet *and* stay safe? At a time when the media is spitting up a terrifying new headline every day about the dangers waiting for young people online, advice to parents is still often narrowly focused on restrictive measures such as delaying access to the internet.

At the same time, whether it's online homework, ed tech learning platforms like Google Classroom at school, parents' WhatsApp groups or family gaming sessions, digital technology is now thoroughly embedded in the routines of family life. You would certainly have to be pretty eccentric, and determined, to avoid it. And you may even be putting kids at a disadvantage if you do. In fact, much rhetoric from the government and the media makes the case for tech skills and digital literacy as essential to young people's future economic well-being in a jobs market we are told will be dominated by STEM and AI industries.[6]

Parents are receiving mixed messages about the risks and benefits of online access for their children. On one hand, they are told by schools and other institutions to make sure they future-proof their kids' tech skills: equip them with laptops, broadband and the latest devices to support their interests and learning. On the other, the government has conceded that the reality of internet harms to kids is such that they must potentially be banned entirely from social media. In the meantime, parents risk being judged neglectful if they don't actively and intensively police their children's internet use. Professor Sonia Livingstone, a leading expert on families' use of technology, calls this 'the digital burden' – a new, and onerous, area of responsibility for parents, many of whom are already reeling and overstretched from the quick successive shocks of the pandemic, a cost of living crisis and, now, tech fears.[7]

Such is the pitch of anxiety at the time of writing, that the UK government, responding to a nationwide public consultation and the influence of energetic parent campaign groups like Smartphone Free Childhood, has moved in favour of an Australian style social media ban for under-sixteens. This measure has been prompted by growing fears about boys' exposure to online misogyny, as well as other internet horrors: cyberbullying, grooming, sextortion, porn, many of which we have touched on in this book.

Current debates that position tech as (simultaneously) a dangerous force to be legislated and controlled *and* the future source of our children's financial success in an economically turbulent world are confusing, to say the least, for your average parent. So, what's the answer? As governments put pressure on the tech giants to remove the features that we know are driving compulsive behaviour, as well as gendered harms and radicalisation, do we also need to find a new way to parent to suit the digital age?

The End of Screen Time

In many ways, parenting has become much more demanding over the last half-century. Despite time pressures in households where often both parents work, mums and dads are involved in their children's lives to a much greater degree now than they were, even in Matteo's 1990s/2000s childhood. Studies show modern parents spend as much as double the time on childcare as those in the 1950s, with fathers, in particular, much more significantly involved than they once were.[8]

Being perceived as a 'good parent' has become a socially desirable aspiration. The social media age has accentuated a competitive spirit among parents which has probably always existed, with ordinary users and 'mumfluencers' alike posting images of harmonious family life and high-achieving kids. Modern parenting has also been criticised as over-protective. According to some commentators, like Jonathan Haidt, author of *The Anxious Generation*, 'helicopter' or 'intensive' parenting has gone too far and is stifling young people's independence.[9] Statistics such as that one in four Gen Z job applicants have supposedly brought a parent along to an interview lend weight to this theory.[10]

However, this increasing involvement in their kids' lives has not yet, for many parents, extended to the digital realm. Research from 2022 found that 66 per cent of parents feel parenting is harder than twenty years ago, with many giving tech as the reason.[11] The promise of tech is that it makes life easier. And there can be no doubt that in many ways it has made the frantic business of modern parenting faster and freer from friction – whether communicating with school and other parents, seeking advice, last-minute school uniform shopping or keeping the kids entertained when you're trying to do some housework.

But the collaborative modern model of authoritative parenting, while it may work well when it comes to, say, promoting good behaviour at mealtimes or encouraging kids to do chores, does not seem as well suited to managing children's use of the internet. It's hard to manifest the parental authority to persuade your child that they have had enough iPad time, for example, when they can clearly see you are glued to your own phone (even if you are just doing the weekly online shop).

Children can easily recognise the hypocrisy in a lot of parents' restrictive practices relating to the use of technology. Additionally, when parents' own digital literacy is lacking, they may find themselves trying to police platforms, devices and online activity which they don't fully understand or are simply unaware of. A study of parents' media literacy, published in 2026, found there was a gulf between parents' understanding and the reality of the content young people are exposed to online. While 80 per cent of parents said they knew which online platforms their child used, only 24 per cent felt very confident they knew what their children were viewing there. Additionally, fewer than half of kids had spoken to their parents about worrying online experiences.[12]

Back when Amelia's son PJ was a kid in the 2010s, there was no blueprint for how to prepare your kids for online life, beyond the generalised mantra of restricting 'screen time'. Children's time in front of screens was considered by parents and the world at large alike to be universally bad – whether TV, video games or the internet. It was treated in the same way as sweets – something to be strictly limited and used as a reward or a privilege. The focus was on the amount of time children spent looking at screens, rather than what they were actually seeing or doing on them.

More than a decade later, parents are still receiving the message that, rather than taking a closer look at the content their kids are interacting with, 'screen time' is the single most important metric they should be tracking as they manage their child's internet use. We know this because they castigate themselves when they think they are failing to limit it. One parent quoted by researchers looking at how tech is integrated into family life was typical, saying she felt 'guilty' and 'lazy' when she let young children watch CBeebies on an iPad in the early morning in order to catch up on her own sleep.[13] A quick glance at the UK's biggest parenting website, Mumsnet, finds lively judgement of a mother who posts that 'screen time' concerns might be overblown, with one parent scolding: 'My DC [darling children] do not have screens, they watch TV, build Lego, do puzzles (physical ones and puzzle books), read books, play board games, ride bikes, play in the garden, etc. You are using screens as a lazy means of childcare and babysitting, you could easily find them other things to do.'[14]

In 2026, the UK government introduced updated recommendations on screen time for very young children, with the prime minister acknowledging: 'It is clear that for years [parents] have been left to wade through conflicting advice and guidance on screen time.'[15] But we actually think the idea that the time a child spends in front of a screen is 'harmful by default' is outdated and largely unhelpful for parents of older kids.[16] It's time to retire it. Firstly, it's ineffective. Children's screen time has been on an upwards trajectory for years as the age for first mobile phone ownership goes down. In 2025, 91 per cent of children owned their own phone by the age of eleven,[17] and most were spending three to four hours a day online. Thirteen- to fourteen-year-olds were averaging four hours on screens, not counting gaming. This trend holds true for adults too of course, whose surfing exceeds their kids' on average.[18]

Secondly, trying to restrict their children's time online is a daily energy-sapping battle for many parents which introduces tension into the family dynamic. Parents are under pressure from peers and professionals to introduce strict rules and restrictions, but kids raised in more 'democratic' modern families often feel empowered to challenge the shaky logic behind them. We adults lack authority in this discussion as kids can see for themselves that we aren't practising what we preach. The result is endless wheedling negotiations. Digital parenting experts Sonia Livingstone and Alicia Blum-Ross have described screen time as: 'a new rod for parents' backs'.[19]

And finally, limiting screen time is a blunt instrument which doesn't take into account how embedded tech is in kids' lives and the many positive opportunities it brings. Kids may be using their screen time to chat with friends, for example, with studies showing that kids who connect online enjoy better friendships in real life.[20] Remember PJ's reflection that his parents' arbitrary 'no gaming on weeknights' rule made him feel left out of his peer community at school? Children use screens for communication, homework research, to explore their creativity through art, music and video creation, and to pursue their hobbies. We think bringing all these things under the one-stop shop of 'screen time' is draconian and doesn't reflect the reality of how we all live now.

Now, we fully accept that at this point in the book, having learned about the many nefarious online actors seeking to poison your son's mind with misogyny, you'll probably be keen to turn the internet off entirely. And, if screen time rules are unrealistic and parental tools are only partly effective and may backfire anyway, causing kids to behave secretively, what's left? Well, luckily, with the benefit of some cutting-edge research, Amelia's hindsight and Matteo's media literacy expertise, we do think we can find a pragmatic way forward, regardless of what happens on a wider societal level in respect of tech regulation and phone bans.

A Note on Parental Controls

Managing a child's digital world can feel overwhelming, not to mention time-consuming. A survey for Parent Zone of the eight largest tech platforms found no fewer than 121 parental tools, which would take seven hours to set up if you activated them all.[21] Nonetheless, parental controls are vital for parents of younger kids who want to minimise the chances of them being exposed to harmful or unsuitable content like porn. The best approach here is to layer protection, creating many safety nets, as shown in the table below.

Layer	Focus Area	How to Implement
Network	Home broadband	Log into your router settings or ISP account (e.g. Sky, BT, Virgin) to turn on **network level filters**. This blocks adult content for every device connected to your Wi-Fi.
Device	Hardware control	Enable 'Screen Time' (iOS) or 'Family Link' (Android). Set devices to 'Ask to buy/ download', so no news apps can be installed without a notification to your phone.
Platform	App-specific settings	Adjust the settings of individual apps (YouTube Kids, Netflix, TikTok). Set age ratings and restricted modes within each ecosystem.

A few extra tips and tricks:

- Smart TVs are often overlooked. Ensure streaming services have PIN protected parental controls.
- Create an admin account for parents on shared home PCs, with a separate user account for each child which prevents them from installing software and does not allow downloads.
- Apps like Discord and Instagram have their own built-in browsers which standard web filters sometimes cannot penetrate.
- Keep in mind that while mobile networks usually filter adult content by default, you often need to manually opt in through your broadband provider to safeguard your home Wi-Fi.
- Filter protections may fail if your child switches to another network or a neighbour's Wi-Fi.
- Check for updates. Security patches and new filter categories are released frequently. Ensure all devices and apps stay updated.
- Review permissions. Regularly check your child's devices to ensure no 'hidden' apps have been installed.

When it comes to teens who are likely to be using social media outside of the home, parental controls guidance becomes more difficult to navigate. Teenagers' growing independence may also lead them to feel resentful about parental surveillance and they can be expert at evading physical controls, finding their own tech solutions to hide activities they don't want their parents to know about. The rise of the 'finsta' (fake Instagram) account among teenagers is a case in point.[22]

A New Kind of Parenting

Despite finding themselves in new-found digital parenting territory, we know, both from our own experience and that of friends and family, that parents do make huge efforts to supervise and support their children's online lives. This has been backed up by experts on families' media use, who refer to parents' strategies to manage their kids' interaction with media as 'parental mediation'.[23]

In the age of mobile technology, when so much of our daily lives is 'mediated', this practice is becoming more central to family life. Recent research has shown that parents manage their kids' use of the internet in a wide variety of ways, with data starting to emerge about which are most effective in balancing risk and maximising young people's well-being.[24]

Experts have categorised parental mediation approaches into diverse styles which loosely fall into the camps of: a) 'restrictive' and b) 'enabling'. Parental levels of involvement in these practices also exist on a spectrum, from those who are highly engaged with kids' internet use through to those who are 'digitally uninvolved'.[25]

Restrictive mediation includes:	Enabling mediation includes:
Monitoring your child's phone records or browser history.	Offering children detailed education on potential online harms.

Restrictive mediation includes:	Enabling mediation includes:
Using tracking apps to keep tabs on their whereabouts.	Giving safety guidance and setting up parental controls with explanations and with the kids' own input (where age-appropriate).
Installing parental controls across devices and apps.	Actively researching games, sites and online activities that your child might enjoy and including them in the process.
Restricting or banning your child's use of, or time spent on, certain apps; or imposing an age limit for access to them.	Initiating discussions with your child about what they are seeing online; asking questions and sharing opinions.
Setting screen time limits.	Having regular, proactive conversations about online safety and 'prebunking' harmful online narratives.
Establishing family rules about where devices can and cannot be used.	Involving kids in family conversations about appropriate tech use and actively listening to their suggestions.
Removing or confiscating devices as punishment, or when use appears compulsive or is breaching family rules (sometimes called 'digital grounding').[26]	Drawing up family agreements together about the use of technology at home.
Preventing children from associating with peers whose tech use is not aligned to the family's own practices (for example, no sleepovers where the family is less strict on observing gaming age ratings).	Consuming digital media or gaming together, chatting about the content as you watch, co-creating digital media such as videos or animation.[27]

A further category (and one which has a striking impact on kids' digital well-being) is 'modelling'.[28] This refers to consciously practising the internet habits you'd like to see your child adopt *yourself*. Most parents can recognise that the 'do as I say, not as I do' technique for imposing your will rarely works.

As keen advocates for media literacy and the benefits which the internet offers kids, you will probably not be surprised to learn that we favour the more 'enabling' approaches outlined here. But it's not straightforward. Enabling mediation may prepare children better for their digital future, but it also exposes them to higher levels of risk.[29]

Most parents will find themselves using a blend of different styles which change over time according to a child's age and maturity. Family life is complex and sometimes messy, with many challenges along the way, from kids' behaviour and mental health to special educational needs – and that is without taking into account other parental stresses such as organising childcare, economic pressures and caring for older relatives. At different times and in diverse contexts, families will need to work out what suits them and their kids best. To the beleaguered Mumsnetter being criticised in the earlier quote, sitting her toddler down with an iPad while she tended to a six-year-old with special needs: we see you, and we acknowledge that you may well have been making the best possible parenting choice at that particular moment of extreme stress.

Parental mediation takes place within many contexts and will also vary according to parents' own digital literacy, their perception of online risk, and how much exposure they are prepared to allow their children. There really is no 'one size fits all' solution, and most mediation of kids' internet use is highly preferable to doing nothing – some experts have argued that 'digitally uninvolved' parents are actually practising a modern-day equivalent of the 'neglectful' style.[30] So let's take a closer look at the kinds of mediation that might best protect young people and influence their long-term digital resilience.

According to the latest research, enabling and restrictive styles of parental mediation both come with varying benefits and drawbacks. The first thing that stands out is that parents' own digital literacy tends to affect their preferred style of mediation: more digitally skilled parents prefer enabling techniques.[31] It makes sense that those who know their way around tech would be more likely to take an active interest in their kids' internet use. Reasonably digitally savvy parents, who know what is lurking out there, are also the most likely to be concerned about digital harms to kids. However, parents with the highest level of technical knowledge may actually somewhat underestimate the level of online risk for their children, as their familiarity with the digital environment may lead to overconfidence.

Parents also appear to have diverging beliefs on how much control they have over their kids' online risks. Parents with a negative attitude towards technology, or who feel 'helpless' and out of control when it comes to managing online risks, prefer to stick to restrictive methods. Conversely, those who feel they can effectively manage kids' exposure to risk and its consequences engage in more active mediation, such as prebunking discussions. However, recent data shows that this does, in fact, result in these parents' more digitally adventurous kids being exposed to more risk.[32]

This is a central paradox of modern digital parenting and one that is at the heart of current debates over teens' access to social media: digital skills and confidence, whether on the part of parents or their kids, do not necessarily reduce risk. Children who are given more freedom to explore the internet will inevitably come across content you'd rather they didn't. However, if they are guided by active parental mediation, they will be better prepared to handle it. It's like controlled exposure to a virus – building up kids' resistance so that once they start to navigate the internet alone, they have the resilience to more confidently negotiate risk.

We think that restrictive mediation is a vital tool in any digital parents' arsenal. It works as an effective shield, particularly for younger kids, against serious harms like exposure to porn, grooming and cyberbullying. But long term, from the research done to date, it does appear to also act as a barrier to children's developing media literacy, one of the reasons why a social media ban alone will never eradicate online harm to kids.[33] Most teenagers are well aware of online harms – how could they not be, given the levels of adult anxiety? They are also concerned by the negative effects of compulsive social media use, which can include impacts on mental health, sleep, and time spent enjoying real-world activities. We need to be enlisting them as co-creators of their own digital well-being, helping us to construct new family rules, norms and agreements which keep them safe from the most serious risks, while respecting their growing independence and agency.

Digital Mentors – The New Authoritative Parent

We are writing this book from opposite ends of the parenting journey. Amelia's son is now grown up and living independently, whereas Matteo is on the front line, juggling toilet training, tantrums and school plays with two little ones. This perspective allows us to look both at the past and into the future as we offer some of our own digital parenting suggestions which might help facilitate healthy internet use and build up boys' emotional resilience to the manosphere mob. We think aspiring to be a kind of 'digital mentor' to your kids is a noble goal which best aligns with the authoritative model of parenting that offers children optimal support. Instead of 'high warmth, high control', we propose 'high engagement, high understanding'. We appreciate that every child and family context is different, so you may want to take a pick-and-mix approach to our advice. That said, here are our thoughts on the strategies that we've found work best for us.

Amelia

In writing this book, my main motivation was to create a resource which I would have found helpful myself when PJ was approaching adolescence. A decade ago, as a busy working parent, my life was jam-packed – as I imagine yours is – with negotiating the logistics of school, work, housework, homework, childcare, shopping, etc., etc. I think it's important to caveat what follows by saying that for the vast majority of us parents, doing what's best for our kids is our primary concern in life. We're just trying to cope as competently as we can with the chaos of family life while passing on our values to our kids and keeping our fingers crossed that they'll turn out happy and successful.

Despite the internet offering many advantages, I agree with the parents quoted in some of the studies we've referred to that it has made parenting tougher. Managing kids' online lives is something that needs to be added to what feels like a never-ending list of parenting tasks – it's time-consuming and takes effort. Looking back on my son's childhood, I can see that our family deployed both 'restrictive' and 'enabling' parental mediation styles, doing some things well and others less so. For what it's worth, I've marked my own homework and offer you the following reflections.

Could do better

- I wish I'd understood more about the nitty-gritty of parental controls and made sure these were optimised across all the family devices. They are complicated to get to grips with, but offer parents important protection against harmful content targeted at kids.
- Having been a keen gamer myself in my teens and twenties who frequently stayed up all night caning the Sega Mega Drive, I was overly fixated on gaming as something that could be addictive, and so strictly controlled the time PJ spent gaming. Matteo has since pointed out to me that playing offline single-player, story-led games is among the safest screen time activities kids can enjoy, as well as developing their imagination and coordination skills.

- More active mediation of PJ's gaming, including paying attention to the kind of games he enjoyed and playing them with him, would have provided more rewarding and moderated screen time for him than the phone surfing which he too often did after school. If you can actively shape your kids' use of the internet by showing them sites, games and activities related to their own interests, you're onto a winner – even more so if you can enjoy them together.
- This leads me on to the wider point about parental assumptions of risk. I assumed that PJ was at risk while gaming, but in fact a single-player video game would have been a safer online environment for him than scrolling YouTube or an apparently 'child-friendly' site like Roblox, which allows user-to-user interactions. It's important to see beyond the brightly coloured graphics and understand as much as you can about the games, platforms and activities your child is engaged in online. You will then be better prepared than I was to mediate their use accordingly.
- Though I was never a huge fan of 'sharenting' (sharing pictures of your kids on social media), one slip-up when I shared a picture of PJ on Twitter (now X) resulted in a cyberbullying incident when school mates discovered the photo online. I would urge all parents to think carefully about putting pictures of their children on the internet apart from on private accounts (even there, with caution). Aside from the very real security concerns this poses, if we want children to understand the rules of consent then we need to respect theirs. If they aren't old enough to give you informed consent to share their photo on social media (an

action which, as of 2026, permits its use in the training of big tech's AI models[34]), why not err on the safe side? More generally, thinking carefully about what you share and always trying to behave respectfully to others online is an important modelling practice too.

- When PJ was in Year Six and started walking to school by himself, we bought him a smartphone as a matter of course, as did the parents of most of his contemporaries. There wasn't the same level of reflection then as now on the wisdom of giving phones to such young children, and if I had the time over, I'd delay it. There is a lot more momentum behind this impulse now, with parents of school peer groups joining forces to make their kids wait. I'd stick to a 'dumb' phone for those early teenage years.
- When I noticed that, as an adolescent, my son was repeating some language and opinions he'd learned from social media, I was alarmed. Sometimes my responses favoured flat contradictions over showing curiosity, or initiating a discussion as an opportunity to find out *why* he was repeating what he'd seen online. I recognise now that, while understandable, this strategy is not effective at countering online misinformation and may even backfire, causing kids to double down on their views.

Gold star

- As a family, we always set rules around the use of devices. Crucially, these were observed by all of us, not just PJ. There is solid evidence that excessive phone use leads to poorer sleep habits, so, right up until PJ left home for uni, we always left all devices downstairs charging overnight.[35] We used old-fashioned alarm clocks to get up on time. While I can't be sure PJ didn't sometimes venture down in the middle of the night for a quick scroll, the fact that we all stuck to this rule means it was never a big deal, just something we did as a matter of course at bedtime.

- PJ also never had a TV or laptop in his bedroom until the Covid-19 lockdown and home schooling in sixth form made that necessary. He played games and scrolled his phone in our living area where either parent could easily glance over at what he was doing. While I appreciate this may be harder for larger families, I do believe that, for us, keeping online activities largely in shared areas mitigated against any secretive behaviour.
- As a mum who worked in the media, I was active on social media, kept abreast of new apps, features and trends, and read up on the potential pitfalls for kids of different platforms. This knowledge of how the wider world was using tech helped me prepare PJ for what he might encounter there. I practised what I preached when it came to having those prebunking conversations we've talked about in this book.
- Above all, we took pains to create a home environment of open and warm communication. Anything and everything could be discussed at family dinner time, and we made sure PJ knew that if ever he felt troubled by anything, or felt he'd done something wrong, he should open up to us about it, rather than trying to cope by himself or cover it up. If he felt lonely, anxious or angry about something, I'd like to think we knew about it.

Research has shown that parental warmth is strongly correlated to children's online well-being – a stronger predictor than restrictive mediation methods such as surveillance or parental controls.[36] If there's one lesson I'd like to pass on, it's the value of building kids' emotional resilience through regular honest and empathetic conversations.

Matteo

As a millennial parent, I recognise that the generation of parents before us was left unsupported when it came to protecting children from online misinformation, harmful narratives and radicalisation. My concern at the way our information ecosystem was headed was what led me to found Shout Out UK in the first place. Unlike Amelia, I'm not yet in the position to offer you much retrospective digital parenting wisdom – one of my offspring is still at the age when crawling around the living room trying to eat fluff is a preferred activity, and the other is just as interested in teddies' tea parties as screens. However, years spent advocating for media literacy and visiting schools to teach it has, as you can imagine, given me strong ideas on how I'd like to mediate my kids' online lives in future.

- Unlike Amelia, I've always been a parental controls obsessive – it's the essential first defence against bad stuff reaching your kids.
- Bearing in mind that harmful content can easily be accessed on most internet-connected devices in a couple of clicks, my

strategy at the moment is to ensure that my kids' 'screen time' (a term which I fully agree has outlived its usefulness) is spent in a controlled environment. In 2017, journalist James Bridle wrote an article that went viral for its devastating critique of the YouTube Kids app. Bridle showed that the autoplay algorithm was amplifying darkly weird, sometimes violent or sexual video animations using popular kids' characters, such as Lightning McQueen, from the *Cars* movies.[37]

- His piece led to a backlash against YouTube that led them to tighten their moderation somewhat, but, *The New York Times* reported in 2026 that the platform was still serving up poor quality AI slop to children.[38] I'm not going to make any assumptions whatsoever about the safety of YouTube *or* YouTube Kids. Instead, we've opted for a kind of 'walled garden' approach to our kids' video-watching. We download specific curated videos to the family iPad, which my kids use without Wi-Fi connection. This acts as a safe, controlled library that still gives my daughter the impression of choosing her own videos.
- Co-viewing media together as a family, and discussing what we see, is very important for us. I also make sure to follow all the content creators my kids watch (Hello, Miss Rachel!), so I can engage with them myself and monitor what they are producing. Once your kids become teenagers, taking a keen interest in what they are looking at online is useful for staying alert to the views they may be exposed to (as well as keeping up with all that baffling Gen Alpha slang).
- Rather than obsessing over screen time, I focus on the activity my kids are engaged in. For example, I'd rather they

spent three hours playing an educational and fun game like Teach Your Monster to Read, my eldest's current favourite, to two hours mindlessly scrolling short-form videos, which increasingly appear to be negatively affecting children's concentration spans.[39]

- As my kids get older, I'm very much in favour of making family agreements together for how we balance on and offscreen activities. Hopefully, taking a collaborative and empowering approach to how we use tech as a family will establish it as a shared space rather than a battleground.
- Building media literacy is a muscle that needs to be strengthened over time. By giving my kids controlled and supervised exposure to the internet and exploring it with them, rather than imposing blanket restrictions, I plan to build their resilience to the future online risks they encounter.
- Relatedly, we parents need to work on our media literacy and critical thinking too. In February 2026, parents' WhatsApp groups in the UK blew up with panic. A series of viral TikTok posts promoting 'Red v Blue school wars' were encouraging kids from rival postcodes to do battle on the streets. In some cases police were even called to schools. The phenomenon was, in fact, a 'phantom trend', inauthentic online activity which gained brief traction, but didn't translate to any real-world mobilisation. Many adults were clearly not equipped to debunk this content – evidence of what the BBC's misinformation correspondent Marianna Spring called 'the social media gap between children and parents'.[40] The government website has some useful resources to help us ask the right questions about online content.

- Start conversations early. It's hard to talk to kids about some of the scarier content that exists online, but it's an essential protective practice. I want my kids to know they can always talk to me about what's going on online, even if they are worried they have done something wrong. I'm also starting to teach my daughter assertiveness: the understanding that others must respect her boundaries, that no means no, and she is within her rights to stand up to bullying, whether at school or online.
- The same applies to talking about sex, relationships and consent more explicitly. If you don't start early, you may find out that a misogynist influencer (or a porn website) has got there first. You can find resources at the back of the book to help you tackle these topics with kids in a reassuring way.
- In 2025, Catherine, Princess of Wales wrote an essay with Professor Robert Waldinger for her Royal Foundation Centre for Early Childhood to draw attention to the impact of what he calls 'technoference': the disruption to the close parent–child connection in daily life caused by parents' distraction by digital devices.[41] In the interests of building a strong and trusting parental bond which reinforces my kids' emotional resilience, I do my best to be fully present for them when we are together – no 'phubbing' (snubbing those you're with while looking at your phone!) for me![42]
- And finally, no phones in the bedroom, ever!

The tech companies' rapid and relentless commercialisation of the most-used online spaces has made keeping children safe a tough task. Thanks largely to the courage and campaigning of bereaved parents pushing for change, it looks as if the tide is set to turn. We hope that future generations will benefit from a carefully regulated 'safety by design' approach by those who construct our digital environment.

Until then, we must face the reality that our kids will not be able to entirely escape seeing harmful content, which will most likely include some expressing dangerous views towards women and girls. We are both, like most people, imperfect parents. But we believe that to prepare children for this eventuality, we must talk about both the good and bad of the digital world with them from an early age.

It's important to remember that no two families are alike. Every parent is juggling different circumstances, pressures and worries. While we are confident that the systemic change needed to keep kids safe online will eventually come, media literacy skills last a lifetime and will reinforce every family's well-being. We hope you will adopt and adapt the tools and strategies we've explored in this book in a way which will positively contribute to your own unique version of family life. If, as parents, we pledge to set firm boundaries together on family internet use, work on our own digital and media literacy, and above all, cultivate a parent–child relationship based on trust, mutual respect and emotional safety, we will be doing our utmost to prepare kids for their online futures.

Conclusion

'The thing that changed for me, looking back at Earth, was that I found myself noticing not only the beauty of Earth, but how much blackness there was around it and how it just made it even more special. It truly emphasised how alike we are, how the same thing keeps every single person on planet Earth alive. We evolved on the same planet, and we have some shared things about how we love and live that are just universal.' – Christina Koch, NASA astronaut and the first woman to travel around the moon as one of the *Artemis II* crew, April 2026[1]

As we finish writing this book, with the NASA astronauts about to touch back down on earth after their historic mission, Christina Koch's powerful words remind us of all we have in common, and of how essential it is to build a sustainable future for the young people of our planet. One of Matteo's daughter's favourite picture books is called, *I Love You to the Moon and Back*, and she has been gripped by the astronauts' progress and every fascinating detail of life onboard their vessel. Just a short while ago, it would have been impossible to imagine that a little girl might one day grow up to be an astronaut like Christina, perhaps inspiring others to do likewise.

We wrote this book because we weren't prepared to sit on the sidelines while noxious voices on the internet declared that girls and women were not worthy of equality and respect. Men and women are spinning through space together, facing the same huge challenges to our world posed by the climate emergency, war and poverty. Our young people face an uncertain future. Doubtless many generations of parents have felt the same thing, but there is no denying that powerful forces of transformation are sweeping the globe as we approach the fourth decade of the twenty-first century. For the human race to survive and thrive, we urgently need to unite. Surely the least we can do is to make sure no one is prevented from achieving their full potential in life on account of their gender.

Access to the internet and digital communication has improved our lives in many ways, from knowledge-seeking to keeping in touch with friends and family and being able to work or study remotely. But the vast explosion of information that we each encounter every day in the aggressively commercial digital environment means that those who own the platforms are desperate to capture and keep our attention at any cost. Sadly, as we learn more and more about the various digital harms unfolding in our societies, one of those costs appears to have been our children's well-being.

There are signs that the tide is turning as people reflect on the damage that has already been done to young people's mental health, as well as our overall societal resilience. UK data shows children and young people are posting less on social media every year and are reporting more negative feelings about their time spent on it – in some cases frustrated by their own addiction to 'brain rot'.[2] The girls we spoke to earlier in the book were mindful of the sexist backlash which might greet their every post, and some were dialling down their online activity as a result.

In March 2026, Meta and YouTube were found liable in a landmark trial in the US for building addictive features which the companies' management *knew* caused harm (in the case in question, harm to the mental health of a young woman, known as 'Kaley', which began in childhood).[3] Some experts described this as a 'big tobacco moment', a tipping point where the law finally caught up with corporate power.[4] As public pressure grows for tighter tech regulation and safer design features for child users, we are hopeful that the grip these platforms hold over teenagers' lives looks set to weaken further.

While the UK government's plans to ban children under sixteen from social media will certainly reduce some harmful content from reaching kids, it can never be failsafe. We think it is important to reframe the debate away from merely banning children from interacting online and towards constructing a safer digital environment worthy of their participation. It need not be inevitable that every time a young person goes online they are confronted with content which showcases hatred, prejudice and violence. These platforms can and should do better. Children and young people are now heading up campaigning movements to put pressure on governments, businesses and judiciaries to hold tech companies to account and build a future technological infrastructure which has their best interests foremost.

Across Europe, youth-led tech justice movements, such as ctrl+alt+reclaim, the Log Off movement, and the UK's own FlippGen, are at the forefront of what we both hope will be a wholesale reimagining and democratising of the internet.[5] Their work is matched by a host of organisations working with boys and young men to promote more inclusive and positive models of masculinity, such as Beyond Equality, which trains university-aged men to facilitate sessions for younger boys in a peer mentoring scheme, and White Ribbon UK, which encourages young men to pledge never to excuse or remain silent about misogyny when they witness it.

We'd like to imagine a future where Matteo's kids will not have to come of age, as Amelia's son and his friends did, on social media platforms where hate and misogyny are normalised and amplified to the extent that a book like the one you have just read was considered necessary. Today's boys and young men are not to blame for the fact that they are exposed to material engineered to anger and radicalise them, and they do not deserve to be stigmatised en masse. But we, as adults, need to show them alternative ways to exist in the world as men, opening up a future where every boy can feel 'man enough' without needing to dominate or denigrate others.

We must all now take responsibility to ensure that the vital progress humanity has made towards gender equality is not irreparably damaged. We owe it to all our children to challenge gender stereotypes which hold us back.

We are hoping for a world where children's online lives are safely regulated, and where they are able to make the best use of the internet's affordances in spaces where misinformation and hate speech are marginalised. But we also need to make sure that if they do encounter it, the next generation will be properly equipped with the vital media literacy skills needed to prebunk and debunk harmful misinformation. We have hope in a future where teaching the prebunking skills in this book to kids will be as routine as teaching them road safety. We are convinced that the population-level adoption of these tools will bring about new cultural norms where boys and girls feel confident to debate robustly – respecting others' opinions, but challenging harmful, degrading or dehumanising misinformation wherever they find it.

This may all sound like an unrealistic dream, when frightening headlines suggest an increasingly polarised digital future for our youth. But we are both media literacy experts, drawn to our chosen field by a belief in the power of communication as a force for good. If we work together to teach boys about the impact of misogyny on women and girls and how it limits their own lives, to promote respectful and meaningful online conversations among young people about the issues that affect them, and to improve the quality of our information environment, we will discover a brighter future for us all.

Thank you for travelling with us, if not to the far side of the moon then, at least, to the end of this book. The fact you've joined us here shows that change is happening. We know that we are far from alone in wishing for a better world for our kids, one where we take even greater leaps towards equality. Let's start now.

Resources for Parents

All details accurate as of March 2026

Promoting Gender Equality and Countering Online Misogyny

SOUK vs the Manosphere. A free guide for parents on talking to boys about online misogyny, featuring the prebunking techniques from this book.

UN Women Same Side Conversation Guide (campaign.unwomenuk.org/same-side). A useful and accessible guide to having open conversations with boys about misogyny and its impact, and why gender equality benefits them too.

Equimundo Global Boyhood Initiative (boyhoodinitiative.org). This site has a wide range of resources for parents and carers to help boys lead happier lives, including advice on how to share their emotions healthily, speak out against bullying and inequality, and break free from restrictive gender stereotypes. Equimundo's main website (equimundo.org/resources) and GBI's Instagram (instagram.com/boyhoodinitiative) carry frequently updated educational materials, blogs, news, and conversation starters.

Thinkuknow (ceopeducation.co.uk). Age-appropriate activities to discuss sensitive issues with boys including porn, sexuality, sextortion and healthy relationships.

Beyond Equality Parents' Toolkit (beyondequality.org/blog-posts/parents-toolkit-talking-with-our-teen-sons). A helpful toolkit for parents on talking to boys about online influencers.

Male Allies UK (maleallies.co.uk/blog) has a regular blog exploring allyship with a focus on the benefits of gender equality for both women *and* men.

White Ribbon UK (whiteribbon.org.uk) is the leading charity in England and Wales engaging men and boys to prevent violence against women and girls.

Online Safety

The UK government's extensive Kids' Online Safety parenting hub (kidsonlinesafety.campaign.gov.uk) carries free resources for parents on a wide variety of topics relevant to the subject matter of this book, including:

- understanding critical thinking,
- finding the right questions to ask children about their online lives,
- how to support children by having content chats every week,
- how to spot misleading or false content,
- how to talk about algorithms.

Quizzes and games are also available from the site, so you can test knowledge together as you learn.

Primary Online Safety, BBC Bitesize (bbc.co.uk/teach/topics/cp44onjz78zt). The BBC's online safety mini site has a wealth of information and videos on a wide variety of topics relating to children's digital lives, including managing friendships online, safety while gaming and much more.

Internet Matters (internetmatters.org). Find information and safety settings for your child's devices and apps, along with guidance to tackle online issues they may face. The website also has a handy step-by-step guide (internetmatters.org/set-upsafe) to layering parental controls for maximum safety.

Cyber Safe Kids (cybersafekids.ie). Ireland's online safety charity's website carries a wealth of resources including sample parental agreements on tech use. Its Same Rules Apply campaign (cybersafekids.ie/samerulesapply) is focused on encouraging responsible parental modelling.

The CEOP website (ceopeducation.co.uk/11_18/lets-talk-about/online-safety/reporting-and-blocking) has a regularly updated guide to how to report and block on social media.

Online Safety Training from the NSPCC (learning.nspcc.org.uk/training/online-safety). Free guides and paid online safety courses.

What I wish my parents or carers knew (childrenscommissioner.gov.uk). A guide from the office of the Children's Commissioner to managing children's digital lives, with accompanying downloadable activity packs, conversation starters and checklists.

Moneyhelper (moneyhelper.org.uk). A service provided by the Money and Pensions Service with advice on how to teach children about online scams and in-app purchasing.

Parental Control Software

It is wise to place parental controls on all devices that your child uses that can access the internet. This includes shared family computers, laptops, phones and iPads. It is vital to have an open and respectful dialogue with your child before implementing parental controls.

Parental controls can:

- filter and block content,
- monitor activity,
- report and alert parents,
- limit time.

Popular software:

- Aura
- Bark
- Norton Family
- Qustodio
- Google Family Link

Tech Radar's website (techradar.com/uk) has regularly updated reviews of all kinds of tech, including parental control apps, dumbphones and safety-modified smartphones.

ParentShield (parentshield.co.uk) is a mobile network specifically designed for children and vulnerable users. Unlike standard networks, it gives parents and carers total visibility and control over the phone's activity.

Bear in mind that if a teen perceives parental controls to be too overbearing, or thinks their privacy is being invaded, they might try to override them or find an alternative way of accessing unfiltered online content. A relationship of mutual trust will protect them from online harm just as much as any software.

Smartphone Free Childhood (smartphonefreechildhood.org) reviews the safest phones for kids on their YouTube channel (youtube.com/watch?v=jF2LHiOPm7M).

Media Literacy

Shout Out UK (shoutoutuk.org/resources). A range of free media literacy resources aimed at children and young people.

Internet Matters (internetmatters.org). Step-by-step safety advice to help manage online use and discuss harmful content with kids and teens.

Parent Zone (parentzone.org.uk). Articles, videos and podcast episodes with advice for parents.

Commonsense Media (commonsense.org/education/family-engagement). The family resources pages of the website provide media literacy tools to help families reinforce critical thinking, creativity, connection and curiosity.

Dismiss (shoutoutuk.org/dismiss). A suite of images and videos prebunking disinformation tactics, aimed at young people.

BBC Verify (bbc.co.uk/news/bbcverify). A team of BBC journalists working to fact-check online news stories and claims and monitor and debunk mis- and disinformation.

Full Fact (fullfact.org). An independent charity which fact-checks claims made by politicians, companies and institutions to counter misinformation.

Preventing and Countering Extremism

ACT Early (actearly.uk). Resources, advice and a confidential support line to discuss and get help for vulnerable individuals.

Educate Against Hate (educateagainsthate.com/parents). Advice, support and FAQs for parents about online safeguarding and having difficult conversations with children.

Pathways game (shoutoutuk.org/pathways). A free youth-centred interactive learning package for education on extremism, radicalisation and Prevent.

Centre for Countering Digital Hate (counterhate.com/parents-guide-how-to-navigate-social-media-safely-with-your-kids). A free guide for parents on helping children navigate social media safely.

Prevent (gov.uk/guidance/making-a-referral-to-prevent). For advice and possibly to make a referral.

Serious Concerns of Harm or Abuse

National Crime Agency CEOP (ceop.police.uk). Report online grooming, sexual abuse or unsafe contact.

Refuge (nationaldahelpline.org.uk; 0808 2000 247). Twenty-four-hour helpline for anyone experiencing abuse or harassment.

NSPCC helpline (nspcc.org.uk/about-us/our-services/nspcc-helpline). To report experiences of sexual harassment and abuse in school call 0800 138 663.

Internet Watch Foundation (iwf.org.uk). Report online child sexual abuse images and videos anonymously here.

Report Remove (childline.org.uk/info-advice/bullying-abuse-safety/online-mobile-safety/report-remove). Tool to help young people under eighteen in the UK confidentially report sexual images and videos of themselves and remove them from the internet.

BEAT (beateatingdisorders.org.uk). Eating disorder support and advice. Use this link to find phone numbers for England, Scotland, Wales and Northern Ireland.

Mental Health Support

Young Minds helpline (youngminds.org.uk/young-person; 0808 802 5544). Advice for parents supporting children with anxiety or low mood.

The Mix (themix.org.uk). Support for under-twenty-fives on any issue.

Molly Rose Foundation (mollyrosefoundation.org/get-support/support-for-parents). Practical guidance for parents on recognising signs that your child might be struggling, understanding the impact of online content and algorithms on their well-being, and knowing what to do if you are worried about suicide or self-harm.

Samaritans (samaritans.org; 116 123). Twenty-four-hour emotional support.

Childline (childline.org.uk; 0800 1111). Free counselling and support for children and young people.

Podcasts

About the Boys. BBC podcast series featuring interviews with boys about their lives today.

Media Minded. Shout Out UK podcast. Five seasons covering online misogyny, conspiracy theories and prebunking and debunking techniques.

To Be a Boy. Lively podcast aimed at parents and carers tackling masculinity and boyhood. The hosts explore male friendships, educational gaps, mental health struggles, and tough topics like male violence.

Tech Shock. Parent Zone podcast covering all aspects of tech and family life with a range of expert guests.

Talking about Sex, Relationships and Porn

CEOP (ceopeducation.co.uk/parents/ask-the-awkward). The National Crime Agency's #AsktheAwkward campaign includes short videos and conversation starters to tackle talking to kids about online pressures and pornography.

Brook (brook.org.uk/parents-and-carers). The UK's leading sexual health charity for young people has an excellent 'Health and Advice for Parents' section.

Further Reading

Laura Bates, *Men Who Hate Women* (Simon & Schuster, 2021)
Laura Bates, *The New Age of Sexism* (Simon & Schuster, 2026)
James Bloodworth, *Lost Boys* (Atlantic, 2025)
Jess Davies, *No One Wants to See Your D*ck* (Headline, 2025)
Lise Eliot, *Pink Brain, Blue Brain* (Oneworld, 2012)
Adele Faber and Elaine Mazlish, *How to Talk so Kids Will Listen and Listen so Kids Will Talk* (Lagom, 2022)
Cordelia Fine, *Delusions of Gender* (Icon, 2011)
Jonathan Haidt, *The Anxious Generation* (Penguin, 2024)
bell hooks, *The Will to Change* (Washington Square Press, 2004)
Jackson Katz, *Every Man* (Penguin, 2025)
Dan Kindlon and Michael Thompson, *Raising Cain* (Ballantine, 2000)
Sonia Livingstone and Alicia Blum-Ross, *Parenting for a Digital Future* (OUP, 2020)
Kate Manne, *Down Girl* (OUP, 2017)
Meadhbh Park, *Blackpilled* (Biteback, 2025)
Richard V. Reeves, *Of Boys and Men* (Swift Press, 2022)
Kaitlyn Regehr, *Smartphone Nation* (Bluebird, 2025)
Angela Saini, *The Patriarchs* (Fourth Estate, 2023)
Jamie Tahsin and Matt Shea, *Clown World* (Quercus, 2024)

Acknowledgements

From both of us:
This book would not have been possible without the many insights of the scholars, journalists and campaigners who have expanded our understanding of misogyny and done so much to expose the underbelly of the contemporary manosphere: among them Laura Bates, James Bloodworth, Alex Blower, Julia Ebner, Debbie Ging, Kate Manne, Meadhbh Park, Jon Rainford, Marianna Spring, Jamie Tahsin and Matt Shea, and Chloe Walsh, the original architect of Shout Out UK's anti-misogyny work.

We are also hugely grateful for the work of Dame Rachel de Souza, the Children's Commissioner for England, Alicia Blum-Ross, Ellen J. Helsper, Sonia Livingstone, Equimundo, Commonsense Media, Sarah Sternberg, and all on the Movember Reimagining Masculinities team and the Centre for Policy Research on Men and Boys. We'd like to thank our friends from fellow organisations in the Online Safety Act Network and the Media and Information Literary Alliance for their much-appreciated support. We are proud to stand with you to advocate for media literacy and a healthier internet for all. Thank you also to the members of the APPG on Political and Media Literacy who continue to advocate in both Houses of Parliament for the importance of this work, and to Dr. James Weinberg and the other members of the APPG's Academic Advisory Group, for their continued support and their scholarly contributions to the growing evidence base for the importance of political and media literacy.

Our team at Shout Out UK is nothing short of epic. They have coped so brilliantly with two of their senior managers taking time out to write a book during the last couple of incredibly hectic years for the organisation. Every day, they are out there at the sharp end, delivering and lobbying for political and media literacy for kids and young people, at a time when it has never been needed more. They are the most committed, clever and funny people we could ever hope to work with. Thank you, you all rock.

We'd like to thank all our interviewees for their time and insights, particularly Calum Jackson. We also owe huge gratitude to our researchers and fact-checkers, Will Callard, Dr Lily Gibbs and Pierre Reutenauer, and to our copy-editor Sam Matthews and proofreader Jane Howard. The combined efforts of this crack team strengthened the manuscript immeasurably. Any data cherry-picking, errors or inconsistencies that remain are entirely the authors' responsibility.

We'd like to thank the team at Souvenir Press. What a joy it has been to work with such an efficient, professional and dedicated team. We are massively grateful for the work of Steve Coventry-Panton on the cover; to Claire Beaumont and her sales team; to Alison Alexanian, Laina Deene, Rosie Parnham and Robert Lokyo Greer in the publicity and marketing departments; and to Emily Frisella in managing editorial.

To Cindy Chan and Mia Cameron: We did it! Many, many, many thanks to you both for your editorial excellence and expert shaping of our manuscript – not to mention your commitment to our mission. We owe this book to you both.

To Rebecca Gray, thank you for believing in us and breathing life into this book.

From Amelia:

Thank you to my family for supporting me, especially my wonderful husband, who is a shining role model of positive masculinity if ever there was one!

Thank you to my incredible tutors on the University of Westminster's Masters course in Communications and Social Change who kick-started my social impact career journey: Anastasia Kavada and Michaela O'Brien.

Thank you to all my pals, who constantly make me laugh and give me hope, especially: all the Slack Captains, Bridget, Jeremy, Tara, Caspian, Helen, Devon, Eva, Jackie, Ethna, Angela, Fil, Katy, Auriol, Suzie, Khrystyna and Daisy.

Thank you to Matteo, for inspiring me every day with your drive for making a difference in the lives of young people, and for the opportunity to write this book together and take our work to the reading public.

From Matteo:

Thank you to my family, especially my incredible partner for supporting me throughout this journey; you are the very epitome of a strong woman, your energy and drive are an inspiration.

Thank you to my mum who moved mountains to give me the best start in life she could.

Thank you to Brunel University for giving me the opportunity to test ideas and begin my journey as a social entrepreneur.

Thank you to Stephen Page and Raj Sharma for taking a chance on a twenty-two-year-old – your investment gave me the opportunity to start this journey. Thank you to James Cathcart, you are the role model who laid the groundwork for the next generation to take up the mantle of this work.

Thank you to my incredible friends who constantly keep me grounded and have always been there through the light and dark: Kiren, Hamza, Joey and Blaychie.

Thank you to Amelia, your expertise and passion challenge me daily, and I wouldn't change it for the world. This book would never have been possible without you, I am forever grateful.

Notes

Introduction

1 Marianna Spring and Mike Radford, 'Meta and TikTok Let Harmful Content Rise After Evidence Outrage Drove Engagement, Say Whistleblowers', BBC News, 16 March 2026.

2 'AI "Aggro-rithms": Young Boys Are Served Harmful Content within 60 Seconds of Being Online', Vodafone UK, press release, 6 February 2024.

3 Written evidence submitted by Hope Not Hate to the Education Committee: Screen Time: Impacts on Education and Wellbeing, UK Parliament, June 2025, committees.parliament.uk/writtenevidence/142884/pdf.

4 *International Women's Day 2026*, Ipsos, 2026, kcl.ac.uk/assets/news/iwd-2026-global-charts-final.pdf.

5 *Review of Sexual Abuse in Schools and Colleges*, Ofsted, 2021.

6 *National Policing Statement 2024 for Violence Against Women and Girls (VAWG)*, National Police Chiefs' Council, July 2024.

7 *Girls' Attitudes Survey 2025: Building a Future Where Girls Belong*, Girlguiding, 2025.

8 'Starmer Announces National Summit on Challenges Facing Men and Boys', ITV News, 19 November 2025.

9 More than 60% of Australian Children Still Using Social Media Despite Ban for Under-16s, Research Shows', Molly Rose Foundation, www.mollyrosefoundation.org/more-than-60-of-australian-children-still-using-social-media-despite-ban-for-under-16s-research-shows/

Chapter 1: Boys are Not the Problem

1 *Children's Involvement in the 2024 Riots*, Children's Commissioner's Office, January 2025, p. 9.

2 'Far Right Movements Behind Rising Tide of Misogyny and Racism in Schools', NASUWT press release, 19 April 2025.

3 *Tackling Violence against Women and Girls*, National Audit Office, 2025, p. 6.

4 Stuart Heritage, 'Is This the Most Terrifying TV Show of Our Times? *Adolescence*, the Drama That Will Horrify All Parents', *Guardian*, 28 February 2025.

5 Jess Phillips, 'Netflix's *Adolescence* Is Not Just a Drama', *Daily Mail*, 15 March 2025.

6 Ian Youngs, '*Adolescence* Hard to Watch as a Dad, Starmer Tells Creators', BBC News, 31 March 2025.
7 Grace Dean, 'Sir Gareth Southgate: Boys Need Role Models Not Gaming and Porn', BBC News, 19 March 2025; *The Richard Dimbleby Lecture: Sir Gareth Southgate*, BBC, 20 March 2025.
8 *Lost Boys: State of the Nation*, Centre for Social Justice, March 2025, p. 7.
9 Nick Hillman and Mark Brooks, *Boys Will Be Boys: The Educational Underachievement of Boys and Young Men*, Higher Education Policy Institute, 2025; *Lost Boys: State of the Nation*, p. 5.
10 *Children and Parents: Media Use and Attitudes Report 2026*, Ofcom, 21 May 2026, p. 4; *'Sex Is Kind of Broken Now': Children and Pornography*, Children's Commissioner's Office, August 2025.
11 *'Sex Is Kind of Broken Now'*, p. 5.
12 Melissa S. de Roos and Emma Ferrando, 'Moderating Effects on the Link between Violent Pornography and Sexual Aggression', *Archives of Sexual Behavior*, 54 (July 2025), p. 2671; *'Sex Is Kind of Broken Now'*; Harriet Smailes, Vanessa. E. Munro and Matt Tonkin, *Strangulation During Sex in the UK*, Institute for Addressing Strangulation, 2025, p. 2.
13 *Lost Boys: State of the Nation*, p. 5.
14 Rosie Campbell et al., *Emerging Tensions? How Younger Generations Are Dividing on Masculinity and Gender Equality*, Ipsos/Policy Institute at King's, 2024, pp. 15, 22, 7.
15 Matthew Smith, 'Young Men, Masculinity and Misogyny', *YouGov*, 14 October 2025.
16 Hillman and Brooks.
17 *Improving School Readiness: Creating a Better Start for London*, Public Health England, 2015; *Early Years Foundation Stage Profile Results: Academic Year 2024/25*, Department for Education, 27 November 2025.
18 *Key Stage 2 Attainment (Revised): Academic Year 2024/25*, Department for Education, December 2025.
19 *Lost Boys: State of the Nation*, p. 20.
20 'Higher Education Student Statistics: UK, 2022/23 – Student Numbers and Characteristics', Statistical Bulletin SB269, HESA, August 2024.
21 'Suspensions and Permanent Exclusions in England: Spring Term 2024–25', Department for Education, 30 April 2026; *Closing the Gender Attainment Gap: Report of Inquiry No. 4: Boys' Educational Underachievement*, All-Party Parliamentary Group on Issues Affecting Men and Boys, November 2023.
22 Hillman and Brooks, p. 10.
23 Jon Andrews and Oana Gavriloiu, 'Level 2 Results Day 2025', Education Policy Institute, 21 August 2025.
24 Hazel Shearing and Hayley Clarke, 'Are Girls Being Left Behind in School? Experts Are Sounding the Alarm', BBC News, 22 August 2025.
25 Diane F. Halpern, Carmen Flores-Mendoza, and Heiner Rindermann, 'Sex, Gender, and Intelligence: Does XX = XY for Intelligence?', in *The Cambridge*

Handbook of the International Psychology of Women, ed. Fanny M. Cheung and Diane F. Halpern (Cambridge, Cambridge University Press, 2020), p. 139.

26 Richard V. Reeves, *Of Boys and Men: Why the Modern Male Is Struggling, Why It Matters, and What to Do about It* (Washington, DC, Brookings Institution Press, 2022).

27 Richard Adams, 'We Need More Male Teachers So British Boys Have Role Models, Says Minister', *Guardian*, 3 April 2025.

28 *Closing the Gender Attainment Gap*, pp. 19–20.

29 Hillman and Brooks, p. 27.

30 *Closing the Gender Attainment Gap*, pp. 45, 43.

31 'The Ten Principles of Taking Boys Seriously', Ulster University, 2025ulster.ac.uk/research/topic/social-work-and-social-policy/research-themes/taking-boys-seriously/steering-group-members/principles.

32 'Ten Principles of Taking Boys Seriously'.

33 Harriet Over et al., 'Understanding the Influence of Online Misogyny in Schools from the Perspective of Teachers', *PLOS One*, 20/2 (February 2025).

34 James Weinberg, *The Missing Link: An Updated Evaluation of the Provision, Practice and Politics of Democratic Education in English Secondary Schools*, Project Report for the All-Party Parliamentary Group on Political Literacy, 2021.

35 Alex Blower and Jon Rainford, *The Problem with Boys? Teachers' Engagement with Masculinity, Mental Health and the Manosphere in the School Classroom*, Boys' Impact, 2025.

36 Christopher McKeon, 'Children to Be Taught How to Resist Andrew Tate "Incel" Culture at School', *Independent*, 15 July 2025.

37 *Lost Boys: State of the Nation*, p. 38.

38 *Active Lives Children and Young People Survey: Academic Year 2024–25 Report*, Sport England, 2025, p. 6.

39 *National Child Measurement Programme (NCMP) annual report, academic year 2024 to 2025, England*, Office for Health Improvement and Disparities, 2025.

40 David M. Duriancik and Courtney R. Goff, 'Children of Single-Parent Households Are at a Higher Risk of Obesity: A Systematic Review', *Journal of Child Health Care*, 23 (September 2019).

41 *Lost Boys: State of the Nation*, p. 48.

42 *State of Play: Interim Report*, Raising the Nation Play Commission, February 2025, p. 27.

43 David Derbyshire, 'How Children Lost the Right to Roam in Four Generations', *Daily Mail*, 15 June 2007.

44 *State of Play*, pp. 12–13.

45 'UK Youth in Direct Call to Government to Realise Benefits of Youth Work', UK Youth, press release, 14 February 2025; 'New UK Government Must Address Play Crisis as a Third of Children in Britain Do Not Have Access to Any Nearby Playgrounds', Fields in Trust, 6 June 2024.

46 Jonathan Haidt, *The Anxious Generation: How the Great Rewiring of Childhood Is Causing an Epidemic of Mental Illness* (London, Allen Lane, 2024).
47 Garrison Wells, Ágnes Romhányi and Constance Steinkuehler, 'Hate Speech and Hate-Based Harassment in Online Games', *Frontiers in Psychology*, 15 (February 2025).
48 'A Digital Playground: The Real Guide to Roblox', Revealing Reality, 13 April 2025, think.revealingreality.co.uk/roblox-real-guide.
49 Steve Sharman et al., 'The National Centre for Gaming Disorders (UK): Who Is Accessing This Service?', *Journal of Behavioral Addictions*, 11/2 (April 2022), p. 147.
50 Haidt, ch. 7.
51 Eleanor Hayward, 'Teenagers' Screen Time Limits Social Skills, Says US Surgeon-General', *The Times*, 1 April 2024.
52 *Generation Isolation 2025: Social Lives, Trust and Connection in an AI Age*, OnSide, 2025, p. 7.
53 Gaby Hinsliff, 'Meet Generation Stay-at-Home: "You Don't Need to Pay to Go Clubbing: You Can Sit at Home and Watch It on Your Phone"', *Guardian*, 10 February 2024.
54 Laura Bates, *Men Who Hate Women: From Incels to Pickup Artists, the Truth about Extreme Misogyny and How It Affects Us All* (London, Simon & Schuster, 2020), pp. 267–9.
55 Marissa Matozzo, 'Gen Z Women Are Choosing Older Men over Guys Their Own Age – and It's Not Because They're Sugar Daddies', *New York Post*, 18 April 2025.
56 *'Sex Is Kind of Broken Now'*, pp. 16, 20, 31, 35.
57 Richie Jones, 'Young Men Believe Women Prioritise Attractiveness and Financial Status When Dating, but Young Women Say Kindness and Humour More Important', Ipsos, 29 May 2025.
58 Sohani Goonetillake, 'One of the Most Popular Apps in the US Is "Fuelling a Gender Divide", Experts Warn', ABC News, 30 August 2025.
59 Jacqui Wakefield, 'My Ex Stalked Me, So I Joined a "Dating Safety" App. Then My Address Was Leaked', BBC News, 23 August 2025.

Chapter 2: The Invisible System

1 Ian Youngs, 'Barbie Overtakes Super Mario Bros to Be 2023's Biggest Box Office Hit', BBC News, 4 September 2023.
2 *Global Gender Gap Report 2025*, World Economic Forum, 2025, p. 5.
3 Isabel Buchanan and Elliot Bridges, *Women in Politics and Public Life*, Research Briefing sn01250, House of Commons Library, 2026, p. 6.
4 'Devastatingly Pervasive: 1 in 3 Women Globally Experience Violence', World Health Organization press release, 9 March 2021.
5 'Violence against Women', World Health Organization fact sheet, 25 March 2024.

6 Simone de Beauvoir, *The Second Sex*, trans. H. M. Parshley (London, Jonathan Cape, 1953).
7 Jordan B. Peterson, *12 Rules for Life: An Antidote to Chaos* (Toronto, Random House Canada, 2018).
8 Yuval Noah Harari, *Sapiens: A Brief History of Humankind* (London, Harvill Secker, 2014), p. 178.
9 Angela Saini, *The Patriarchs: How Men Came to Rule* (London, HarperCollins, 2023).
10 Aristotle, *Generation of Animals*, trans. A. L. Peck (London, Heinemann, 1943), II.iii, p. 175; and *Politics*, trans. H. Rackham (London, Heinemann, 1932).
11 Meilan Solly, 'Researchers Reaffirm Famed Ancient Viking Warrior Was Biologically Female', *Smithsonian Magazine*, 21 February 2019.
12 Peter Caires and Emma Nagouse, based on research by Ronald C. Po, 'Zheng Yi Sao: The Most Successful Pirate in History', BBC Reel, 23 June 2022.
13 Angela Saini, 'How Did Patriarchy Actually Begin?' *BBC Future*, 30 May 2023.
14 'Labour Market Overview, UK: March 2026', Office for National Statistics, 19 March 2026.
15 Kate Manne, *Down Girl: The Logic of Misogyny* (New York, Oxford University Press, 2017), p. 63.
16 Laura Bates, *Men Who Hate Women: From Incels to Pickup Artists, the Truth about Extreme Misogyny and How It Affects Us All* (London, Simon & Schuster, 2020).
17 'Misogyny Resource', Tender, March 2025; Alex Walker et al., 'Preventing Sexual Harassment Through a Prosocial Bystander Campaign: It's #SafeToSay', *Journal of Community Safety and Well-Being*, 8/3 (September 2023).
18 '"Medical Misogyny" Is Leaving Women in Unnecessary Pain and Undiagnosed for Years', House of Commons Women and Equalities Committee, 11 December 2024.
19 Tim Tonkin, 'BMA Aims to End Sexism', BMA News and Opinion, 6 March 2023.
20 Nick Gibb, MP, to Jesse Norman, MP, letter regarding the 'Fertile Heart' curriculum, 7 June 2021, humanists.uk/wp-content/uploads/2021-0019914-Jesse-Norman-Fertile-heart-1.pdf.
21 'Islamic School Segregates and Treats Girls Unfavourably, Says Ofsted', National Secular Society, 8 January 2020.
22 *Girls' Attitudes Survey 2025: Building a Future Where Girls Belong*, Girlguiding, 2025.
23 'Ofsted: Culture Change Needed to Tackle "Normalised" Sexual Harassment in Schools and Colleges', press release, Ofsted, 10 June 2021.
24 Emily Dugan, '"It's Rife": Female MPs Tell of Climate of Misogyny in Westminster', *Guardian*, 29 April 2022.
25 Alex Shepherd et al., *A House for Everyone: A Case for Modernising Parliament*, Fawcett Society, 2023.

26 Dugan.
27 Sima Kotecha, 'Westminster: House of Commons Culture Still "Predatory", Say Staff', BBC News, 5 July 2023.
28 Baroness Casey, *Final Report: An Independent Review into the Standards of Behaviour and Internal Culture of the Metropolitan Police Service*; Vikram Dodd, 'Met Police Found to Be Institutionally Racist, Misogynistic and Homophobic', *Guardian*, 21 March 2023.
29 Iain Overton, 'Second-Class Soldiers: A Culture Audit of the British Army's Enduring Sexism Comes to Light', Action on Armed Violence, 25 July 2025; Ed Halford, 'British Army Accused of Suppressing Report on Barracks Sex Pests', *The Times*, 24 September 2025.
30 Bea Swallow, 'Soldier "Manipulated by Suicide Threat" – Inquest', BBC News, 13 February 2025.
31 Leah Culhane and Andrew Bazeley, *Gender Stereotypes in Early Childhood: A Literature Review*, Fawcett Society, 2019.
32 Lise Eliot, *Pink Brain, Blue Brain: How Small Differences Grow into Troublesome Gaps – And What We Can Do About It* (London, Oneworld Publications, 2009).
33 Culhane and Bazeley.
34 Sebastian Kraemer, 'The Fragile Male', *BMJ*, 321 (23 December 2000), p. 1609.
35 Cordelia Fine, *Delusions of Gender: How Our Minds, Society, and Neurosexism Create Difference* (London, Icon Books, 2010), p. 199.
36 Lucy L. Clarke et al., 'The Gendered Behaviors Displayed by Disney Protagonists', *Frontiers in Sociology*, 9 (6 May 2024), p. 1.
37 Fine.
38 Eliot.
39 Emily R. Mondschein, Karen E. Adolph, and Catherine S. Tamis-LeMonda, 'Gender Bias in Mothers' Expectations about Infant Crawling', *Journal of Experimental Child Psychology*, 77 (December 2000).
40 Elizabeth S. Spelke, 'Sex Differences in Intrinsic Aptitude for Mathematics and Science? A Critical Review', *American Psychologist*, 60 (December 2005).
41 Eliot, p. 77.
42 Culhane Bazeley, p. 23.
43 Katie Pickles, 'In Greta Gerwig's Barbie Land, the Matriarchy Can Be Just as Bad as the Patriarchy', *The Conversation*, 20 July 2023.
44 e.g. Hamza, 'Feminists Are Genuinely Evil', YouTube, 2 November 2024, youtube.com/watch?v=gzoaoyQmETI.
45 Brian Heilman, Gary Barker and Alexander Harrison, *The Man Box: A Study on Being a Young Man in the US, UK, and Mexico*, Equimundo, 2017, p. 15.
46 *International Women's Day 2024: Global Attitudes Towards Gender Equality*, King's College London/Ipsos, 2025, kcl.ac.uk/giwl/assets/iwd-2025-survey.pdf.
47 Heilman, Barker, and Harrison, p. 15.
48 Krista Fisher, Simon Rice and Zac Seidler, *Young Men's Health in a Digital World*, Movember Institute of Men's Health, 2025, pp. 24, 37.

49 Timothy Piatkowski and Samuel Cornell, 'Get Big or Die Trying: Social Media Is Driving Men's Use of Steroids. Here's How to Mitigate the Risks', *The Conversation*, 3 April 2025.
50 Grace Dean, 'These Men Put Off Doctor's Visits Again and Again. Then Came a Tipping Point', BBC News, 21 April 2025.
51 Robert Booth, 'Gen Z Boys and Men More Likely than Baby Boomers to Believe Feminism Harmful, Says Poll', *Guardian*, 1 February 2024.
52 bell hooks, *The Will to Change: Men, Masculinity, and Love* (London, Washington Square Press, 2004), p. 15.
53 Xavier Mulenga, 'Loneliness Is Killing Men – and Without Proper Support and Intervention Nothing Will Change', *Guardian*, 21 July 2024; Benedict Vigers, 'Younger Men in the US Among the Loneliest in West', *Gallup*, 20 May 2025.
54 Margaret E. Greene et al., *Men and Gender Equality: A Global Status Report in 15 Headlines*, Equimundo, 2022.
55 Magdalena Zawisza, 'Study Reveals Gender Equality Benefits Everyone', Anglia Ruskin University News, 10 January 2025.

Chapter 3: The (M)analogue Beginning

1 James Ball and Symeon Brown, 'BBM: The Rioters' Communication Method of Choice', *Guardian*, 7 December 2011.
2 Kathleen Boykin McElhaney et al., 'Attachment and Autonomy During Adolescence', in *Handbook of Adolescent Psychology*, ed. Richard M. Lerner and Laurence Steinberg (Hoboken, NJ, John Wiley & Sons, 2009).
3 Daniel Davies, 'Dating "Expert" Says Men Should Never Let a Woman Pay for the First Date', *Men's Health*, 18 June 2021.
4 Tom Fordy, 'How to Be a Man According to the Characters of BBC's *The Office*', *ShortList*, 6 July 2016.
5 Neil Strauss, *The Game: Undercover in the Secret Society of Pickup Artists* (London, Cannongate Books, 2007).
6 James Bloodworth, *Lost Boys: Undercover in the Manosphere* (London, Atlantic Books, 2025), pp. 6–7.
7 Arie Perliger, Catherine Stevens and Eviane Leidig, *Mapping the Ideological Landscape of Extreme Misogyny*, International Centre for Counter-Terrorism, 2023.
8 Vivian Gerrand et al., 'Mapping the Neo-Manosphere(s): New Directions for Research', *Men and Masculinities* 28 (17 June 2025), p. 443, doi.org/10.1177/1097184X251350277.
9 Michael White, 'Suspend the Rightwing Tory MP Philip Davies? No Way, He'd Love It', *Guardian*, 15 August 2016.
10 'Are Men The Real Victims Of Sexism?', This Morning, *YouTube*, 16 January 2015, youtube.com/watch?v=ybGiOLp3WO8.
11 Perliger, Stevens and Leidig.
12 Perliger, Stevens and Leidig, p. 3.

13 James Crowley, '"The Matrix" Creator Explains What The Red Pill Really Is and Men's Rights Activists Aren't Going to Be Happy', *Newsweek*, 7 August 2020.
14 Meadhbh Park, *Blackpilled: Masculinity, Media and Incels* (London, Biteback Publishing, 2025), p. 29.
15 Brit Dawson, 'Adolescence's 80/20 Rule of Dating Debunked – An Expert Explains Why 80% of Women Fancying Just 20% of Men Is BS', *Cosmopolitan*, 31 March 2025; Written evidence from Jessica Aiston et al. (EOV0019), UK Parliament, September 2023, committees.parliament.uk/writtenevidence/124930/pdf.
16 Stephen Marche, 'Swallowing the Red Pill: A Journey to the Heart of Modern Misogyny', *Guardian*, 14 April 2016.
17 'YouTube U-turn over Red Dead Redemption 2 Suffragette Clips', BBC News, 8 November 2018.
18 Jason Schreier, 'Rockstar Games Cleaned Up Its Frat-Boy Culture – and Grand Theft Auto, Too', *Bloomberg*, 27 July 2022.
19 Laura Bates, *Men Who Hate Women: From Incels to Pickup Artists, the Truth about Extreme Misogyny and How It Affects Us All* (London, Simon & Schuster, 2020), pp. 147–51.
20 Shout Out UK/Matteo Bergamini (host), 'Gamergate: Misogyny Gone Viral', *Media Minded* podcast, s. 2, ep. 6, 10 May 2022.
21 David B. Nieborg and Maxwell Foxman, 'Mainstreaming Misogyny: The Beginning of the End and the End of the Beginning in Gamergate Coverage', in *Mediating Misogyny: Gender, Technology, and Harassment*, ed. Jacqueline Ryan Vickery and Everette E. Everette (Cham, Palgrave Macmillan, 2018), p. 125.
22 Jim Taylor, 'The Woman Who Founded the "Incel" Movement', BBC News, 30 August 2018.
23 Bates, *Men Who Hate Women*, pp. 11–21.
24 Park, p. 217.
25 Bloodworth, p. 225; 'Elliot Rodger: How Misogynist Killer Became "Incel Hero"', BBC News, 26 April 2018.
26 Alexandra Woodward et al., *Incels: Inside the World of Involuntary Celibates*, Manhattan District Attorney's Office/NYU SPS Center for Global Affairs, December 2021.
27 Jessica Elgot and Rajeev Syal, 'Yvette Cooper to Reject Call to Broaden Extremism Definition', *Guardian*, 28 January 2025.
28 Johanna Carr, 'Plymouth Shootings: Why Was Jake Davison Allowed a Gun?' BBC News, 21 February 2023.
29 Dominic Casciani and Daniel De Simone, 'Incels: A New Terror Threat to the UK?' BBC News, 13 August 2021.
30 Ruth Kinane, '*Adolescence*: Everything to Know About the Emmy-Winning One-Shot Crime Drama', Tudum (Netflix), 12 January 2026.
31 Shout Out UK/Matteo Bergamini (host), 'Incels: Swallowing the Black Pill', *Media Minded* podcast, s. 2, ep. 9, 21 June 2022.

32 Joe Whittaker, William Costello and Andrew G. Thomas, *Predicting Harm Among Incels (Involuntary Celibates): The Roles of Mental Health, Ideological Belief and Social Networking*, independent report, Commission for Countering Extremism, 2024, Table 1.

33 Manoel Horta Ribeiro et al., 'The Evolution of the Manosphere Across the Web', *Proceedings of the International AAAI Conference on Web and Social Media*, 15 (2021), p. 197.

34 Bates, *Men Who Hate Women*, p. 95.

35 Laura Bates, 'Men Going Their Own Way: The Rise of a Toxic Male Separatist Movement', *Guardian*, 26 August 2020.

36 'Piers Morgan Mocks Daniel Craig for Carrying Baby', BBC News, 16 October 2018.

37 Bloodworth, p. 97.

38 William Costello et al., 'Levels of Well-being Among Men Who Are Incel (Involuntarily Celibate)', *Evolutionary Psychological Science*, 8 (September 2022).

39 Ren Zhou, 'Understanding the Impact of TikTok's Recommendation Algorithm on User Engagement', *International Journal of Computer Science and Information Technology*, 3/2 (July 2024); Smitha Milli et al., 'Engagement, User Satisfaction, and the Amplification of Divisive Content on Social Media', *PNAS Nexus*, 4/3, (March 2025).

40 Soumya Awasthi, 'From Clicks to Chaos: How Social Media Algorithms Amplify Extremism', Observer Research Foundation, 13 February 2025.

41 *Boys in the Digital Wild: Online Culture, Identity, and Well-being*, Common Sense Media, 2025, pp. 8, 22.

42 Jamie Tahsin and Matt Shea, *Clown World: Four Years Inside Andrew Tate's Manosphere* (London, Quercus, 2024).

43 Shanti Das, 'Inside the Violent, Misogynistic World of TikTok's New Star, Andrew Tate', *Guardian*, 6 August 2022.

44 Kari Paul, '"Dangerous Misogynist" Andrew Tate Removed from Instagram and Facebook', *Guardian*, 19 August 2022.

45 Brock Wilson, 'Andrew Tate's Been Banned from Social Media. But His Harmful Content Still Reaches Young Men', CBC News, 7 September 2022.

46 *Andrew Tate: The Man Who Groomed the World?*, dir. Jamie Tahsin (2023).

47 Rachel Hall, 'Beyond Andrew Tate: The Imitators Who Help Promote Misogyny Online', *Guardian*, 19 March 2025.

48 Gina Neff et al./Minderoo Centre for Technology and Democracy, 'Economies and Structures of Online and Offline Misogyny', written evidence to the House of Commons Women and Equalities Committee inquiry into 'Misogyny: the manosphere and online content' (MIS0042), 6 June 2025, committees.parliament.uk/writtenevidence/142618/pdf.

Chapter 4: Boys Unfiltered

1 Alejandro L. Mujica et al., 'Addiction by Design: Some Dimensions and Challenges of Excessive Social Media Use', *Medical Research Archives*, 10/2 (February 2022).
2 Zoe Taylor, Aliaksandra Yankouskaya and Constantina Panourgia, 'Social Media Use, Loneliness and Psychological Distress in Emerging Adults', *Behaviour and Information Technology*, 43/7 (2024), p. 1312.
3 e.g. Piers Morgan (host), 'Breaking: Andrew Tate On Legal Win "Another Step Closer to Complete Exoneration!"' *Piers Morgan Uncensored* podcast, 29 September 2025.
4 This Instagram clip is the closest we could find to this trope: instagram.com/reels/CZAxVnHlojd.
5 Noor Nanji and Zoe Conway, 'Unions Accuse McDonald's of "Repeated Harassment" against "Mostly Teenage" Staff', BBC News, 8 January 2026.
6 From July 2025, the UK's Online Safety Act required platforms to have stricter age-verification systems in place, with simple 'I am 18' checkboxes no longer sufficient.

Chapter 5: Girls Talking

1 Rachel Connolly, 'Why Fear the Tote Bag-Wielding, Matcha-Drinking "Performative Male"? At Least He Makes an Effort', *Guardian*, 29 August 2025. This article is a good introduction to the idea of the 'performative male'.
2 Constance Beaufils, Heejung Chung and Shiyu Yuan, *Tradwife: Between Myths and Realities*, Global Institute for Women's Leadership, King's College London, 2025, p. 6, kcl.ac.uk/giwl/assets/giwl-tradwife-report.pdf.

Chapter 6: Boys Behind Screens

1 Emma Beddington, 'Is 'Princess Treatment' a Harmless Trend – or More Fuel for Misogyny?' *Guardian*, 4 July 2025.
2 Jean Garnett, 'The Trouble with Wanting Men', *The New York Times Magazine*, 21 July 2025.
3 *Delusional Diaries* podcast, instagram.com/p/DPZAcB1jhyq, 4 October 2025.
4 *Children and Parents: Media Use and Attitudes Report*, Ofcom, 7 May 2025, pp. 8, 19.
5 *Boys in the Digital Wild: Online Culture, Identity, and Well-being*, Common Sense Media, 2025, p. 7.
6 *Children and Parents: Media Use and Attitudes Report*, p. 20.
7 Annabel Rackham, 'The Sidemen: Our YouTube Content Lets You Escape', BBC News, 9 September 2023.
8 Manish Pandey, 'Prime Drink: How KSI and Logan Paul Made It So Popular', BBC News, 18 April 2023.
9 Yixuan Li, Zihao Liu and Fangqing Liu, 'Parasocial Relationships with Social

Media Influencers and Mental Health Outcomes: A Systematic Review and Meta-analysis', *JMIR* preprint, 27 March 2026.
10 Harriet Marsden, 'KSI: "Renaissance Man of Digital Age" in Racism Storm', *The Week*, 4 April 2023.
11 Eric Berger, 'Conservative US Lawmakers Are Pushing for an End to No-Fault Divorce', *Guardian*, 25 June 2024.
12 Catherine Baker, Debbie Ging and Maja Brandt Andreasen, *Recommending Toxicity: The Role of Algorithmic Recommender Functions on YouTube Shorts and TikTok in Promoting Male Supremacist Influencers*, summary report, DCU Anti-Bullying Centre, Dublin City University, 2024.
13 Rajeev Syal, 'Police Investigate Ukip Candidate over Jess Phillips Rape Comments', *Guardian*, 7 May 2019.
14 *State of Hate 2026*, Hope Not Hate, 2026, p. 64.
15 Eirian Jane Prosser, 'The Truth About How Much TikTok Influencer Hamza Ahmed Really Earns and His Extraordinary Rise from a VERY Humble Start', *Daily Mail*, 26 August 2025.
16 *Children and Gaming: An Analysis of Parental Attitudes*, Ygam and Mumsnet, 2025, p. 11.
17 Krista Fisher et al., *Young Men's Media Landscaping Report*, Movember Institute of Men's Health, 2025, p. 15.
18 *Children and Gaming*, p. 36.
19 *Boys in the Digital Wild*, p. 18.
20 Cynthia Miller-Idriss, 'Misogyny Incubators: How Gaming Helps Channel Everyday Sexism into Violent Extremism', *Frontiers in Psychology*, 16 (2025).
21 Ed Nightingale, 'Pokimane Leaves Twitch Due to a Rise in "Manosphere, Red Pill Bullsh*t"', Eurogamer, 1 February 2024.
22 *Boys in the Digital Wild*, p. 16.
23 Jessica White et al., *Radicalisation Through Gaming: The Role of Gendered Social Identity*, Whitehall Report 2–24, Royal United Services Institute for Defence and Security Studies, 2024.
24 Mariana Olaizola Rosenblat, *Gaming the System: How Extremists Exploit Gaming Sites and What Can Be Done to Counter Them*, NYU Stern Center for Business and Human Rights, 2023.
25 Julia Ebner, 'Christchurch Shooting: What Terror Looks Like in the Social Media Age', *Sunday Times*, 15 March 2020.
26 Rosenblat, p. 13.
27 Megan Farokhmanesh, 'The Small Company at the Center of "Gamergate 2.0"', Wired, 14 March 2024.
28 *Experiences of Engaging with the Manosphere*, Ofcom/Revealing Reality, 2025, p. 42.
29 Elle Hunt, 'The Disturbing Rise of Clavicular: How a Looksmaxxer Turned His "Horror Story" into Fame', *Guardian*, 18 February 2026.

30 *Boys in the Digital Wild*, p. 6.
31 Alexandra Pattillo, '"Why Are My Biceps So Small?" The Boys and Young Men Turning to Steroids', *Guardian*, 27 December 2024.
32 Krista Fisher et al., *Young Men's Health in a Digital World*, Movember Institute of Men's Health, 2025, p. 4.
33 The National Parent Survey 2025, Parentkind, 2025, p. 94.
34 *'A Lot of It Is Actually Just Abuse': Young People and Pornography*, Children's Commissioner's Office, 2023, pp. 4, 5.
35 *'A Lot of It Is Actually Just Abuse'*, p. 21.
36 Janice Turner, 'Bonnie Blue: 1,000 Men and the Worrying Normalisation of Porn', *The Times*, 25 July 2025.
37 Rob Moore (host), 'Confronting Andrew Tate and Bonnie Blue: World Exclusive: Have Men Lost Their Power and Has Feminism Ruined Society?', *Disruptors* podcast, 20 June 2025.
38 Eoghan Cleary, 'The Porn Industry Is Normalising the Sex Trade for the Next Generation of Teen Girls', *The Journal*, 3 February 2026.
39 *'A Lot of It Is Actually Just Abuse'*, p. 26.
40 'New Evidence on Pornography's Influence on Harmful Sexual Behaviour Among Children', Children's Commissioner's Office, press release, 9 May 2023.
41 Joanne Upton et al., *The Relationship between Pornography Use and Harmful Sexual Attitudes and Behaviours: Literature Review*, Government Equalities Office, 2021.
42 P.H. Bhuptani et al., 'Pornography Use, Perceived Peer Norms, and Attitudes Toward Women: A Study of College Men', *American Journal of Sexuality Education*, 2024, 19/3.
43 Jessica Ringrose, Kaitlyn Regehr, and Betsy Milne, *Understanding and Combatting Youth Experiences of Image-Based Sexual Harassment and Abuse*, University College London, 2021, p. 41.
44 Sean O'Neill, 'Private Schools in Police Inquiry Over Deepfake Porn Images of Girls', *The Times*, 20 June 2024.
45 Tom Gerken, 'Meta Urged to Go Further in Crackdown on "Nudify" Apps', BBC News, 12 June 2025.
46 'Police Action in Response to Youth Produced Sexual Imagery ("Sexting")', briefing note, version 1.0, College of Policing, 2016.
47 *'One Day This Could Happen to Me': Children, Nudification Tools and Sexually Explicit Deepfakes*, Children's Commissioner's Office, 2025, p. 10.
48 Robert Booth, 'Grok AI Generated about 3m Sexualised Images in 11 Days, Study Finds', *Guardian*, 22 January 2026.
49 Jason Parham, 'Confessions of a Recovering AI Porn Addict', Wired, 1 August 2025.
50 Rhitu Chatterjee, 'Teens Are Having Disturbing Interactions with Chatbots. Here's How to Lower the Risks', NPR, 29 December 2025.

51 Tir Dhondy, 'BBC Tracks Down Sextortion Scammer Targeting Teenage Boys', BBC News, 5 October 2025.
52 Adele Robinson, 'Gamifying Abuse: The Sadistic Online Groups Where Children Trade Harmful Content for Status', Sky News, 29 January 2026.
53 Se Youn Park, 'Everyday Extremism: Molka, Nth Room, and the Infrastructure of Digital Misogyny', GNET, 15 October 2025.

Chapter 7: How to Talk so Boys Will Listen

1 Helen Thompson, 'Teenage Girls Have Led Language Innovation for Centuries', *Smithsonian Magazine*, 10 August 2015.
2 Kathleen Boykin McElhaney et al., 'Attachment and Autonomy During Adolescence', in *Handbook of Adolescent Psychology*, ed. Richard M. Lerner and Laurence Steinberg (Hoboken, NJ, John Wiley & Sons, 2009).
3 Tara M. Chaplin and Amelia Aldao, 'Gender Differences in Emotion Expression in Children: A Meta-Analytic Review', *Psychological Bulletin*, 139/4 (2013).
4 Matthew Oransky and Jeanne Marecek, '"I'm Not Going to Be a Girl": Masculinity and Emotions in Boys' Friendships and Peer Groups', *Journal of Adolescent Research*, 24/2 (March 2009).
5 Dan Kindlon and Michael Thompson, *Raising Cain: Protecting the Emotional Life of Boys* (New York, Ballantine Books, 1999), p. 10.
6 *The Voice of the Boys Report: How Boys in Secondary School Education Feel About Being a Boy Today*, Male Allies UK, 2025, p. 5.
7 Ronald F. Levant and Katherine Richmond, 'The Gender Role Strain Paradigm and Masculinity Ideologies', in *The Psychology of Men and Masculinities*, ed. Ronald F. Levant and Y. Joel Wong (Washington, DC, American Psychological Association, 2016).
8 Rune Ellefsen and Sveinung Sandberg, 'Everyday Prevention of Radicalization: The Impacts of Family, Peer, and Police Intervention', *Studies in Conflict and Terrorism*, 47/10 (2024), p. 1348.
9 Kindlon and Thompson, p. 10.
10 Vivian Gerrand et al., 'Mapping the Neo-Manosphere(s): New Directions for Research', *Men and Masculinities*, 28/5 (December 2025).
11 The definitions in this table are based on those used in the EU DigComp 2.2 Framework, https://publications.jrc.ec.europa.eu/repository/handle/JRC128415 and the European Digital Media Observatory guidelines on media literacy, https://digital-strategy.ec.europa.eu/en/policies/media-literacy.
12 Shout Out UK/Matteo Bergamini (host), 'Antisemitism and the Roots of Hate: A Conversation with Former Extremists (Special Episode)', *Media Minded* podcast, s. 2, ep. 8, June 2022.
13 William I. Brustein, *Roots of Hate: Anti-Semitism in Europe before the Holocaust* (Cambridge: Cambridge University Press, 2003).

14 Christian Rudder, 'Your Looks and Your Inbox', OkTrends blog, 17 November 2009, gwern.net/doc/psychology/okcupid/yourlooksandyourinbox.html.
15 Elle Hunt, 'Everyone's so Intolerant Online. Am I Right to Stay Silent?', *Guardian*, 22 May 2024.
16 Sophia Ankel, 'Ex-Moonie Cult Members are Helping Families of QAnon Believers Build Bridges with their Loved Ones', Business Insider, 28 March 2021.
17 Cited in Anand Giridharadas, *The Persuaders: At the Front Lines of the Fight for Hearts, Minds, and Democracy* (New York, Penguin Books, 2023), p. 55.
18 Joseph Grenny et al., *Crucial Conversations: Tools for Talking When Stakes Are High*, 3rd edn (New York, McGraw Hill, 2021).
19 Sophia Ankel, 'Ex-Moonie Cult Members are Helping Families of QAnon Believers Build Bridges with their Loved Ones', Business Insider, 28 March 2021.
20 Shane McCarty et al., 'Bystander Interventions for Promotion and Prevention: Applying Promotion Science, Motivation Science, and Behavioral Science to Upstanding', OSF preprint, 16 August 2022.
21 Jonathan Kenyon, Jens Binder and Christopher Baker-Beall, *The Internet and Radicalisation Pathways: Technological Advances, Relevance of Mental Health and Role of Attackers*, Ministry of Justice Analytical Series, HM Prison and Probation Service, 2022, p. 20.
22 'Signs of Depression in Children and Young People', NHS website, 25 January 2023.

Chapter 8: Parenting 3.0

1 Thomas G. Power, 'Parenting Dimensions and Styles: A Brief History and Recommendations for Future Research', *Childhood Obesity*, 9/1, supplement (August 2013), p. S-14.
2 Gwen Dewar, 'Parenting Styles: An Evidence-based, Cross-cultural Guide', *Parenting Science*, last modified April 2024, parentingscience.com/parenting-styles.
3 'Dealing with Child Behaviour Problems', NHS, 2022, nhs.uk/baby/babys-development/behaviour/dealing-with-child-behaviour-problems.
4 'Research and Background: Parenting and HLE', The National Centre for Family Hubs/Local Government Association, [n.d.].
5 'Technology Has Broken Authoritative Parenting – Here's How We Fix It', Parent Zone, 7 April 2026.
6 Derek Bosworth and Jeisson Cárdenas-Rubio, 'AI Skills for Life and Work: Labour Market and Skills Projections', Department for Science, Innovation and Technology, 28 January 2026.
7 Sonia Livingstone and Alicia Blum-Ross, *Parenting for a Digital Future: How Hopes and Fears Shape Children's Lives* (Oxford, Oxford University Press, 2020), p. 5.

8 Vivek H. Murthy, *Parents Under Pressure: The U.S. Surgeon General's Advisory on the Mental Health and Well-Being of Parents*, Office of the US Surgeon General, 2024.
9 Jonathan Haidt, *The Anxious Generation: How the Great Rewiring of Childhood Is Causing an Epidemic of Mental Illness* (London, Allen Lane, 2024), pp. 71–87.
10 '1 in 4 Gen Zers Brought a Parent to a Job Interview', ResumeTemplates.com, 21 May 2024.
11 Phil Raws, *Net Gains? Young People's Digital Lives and Well-being: A Research Review and New Findings*, Children's Society, 2022, p. 36.
12 *Media Literacy Parents' Study*, YouGov/Department for Science, Innovation and Technology, 2026, pp. 3, 11.
13 Livingstone and Blum-Ross, p. 29.
14 'To Think Current Concerns Over Screen Time Is Bordering Hysteria', Mumsnet AIBU discussion board, 22 January 2026.
15 Keir Starmer, 'Speaking with parents today ...' (Facebook post), 27 March 2026, facebook.com/KeirStarmerLabour/posts/speaking-with-parents-today-it-is-clear-that-for-years-they-have-been-left-to-wa/1539856564178505.
16 'Harmful by default' is Raws's phrase, p. 17.
17 *Children and Parents: Media Use and Attitudes Report*, Ofcom, 7 May 2025, p. 14.
18 'Five Ways to Help Your Teen to Spend Less Time on Their Screens', BBC Bitesize, January 2026.
19 Livingstone and Blum-Ross, p. 33.
20 Raws, p. 17.
21 'Technology Has Broken Authoritative Parenting', Parent Zone.
22 Andrea Chang, 'The Real Truth about Finstagrams and Second Accounts: How Youth Navigate Authenticity on Instagram', Medium, 3 April 2025.
23 Sonia Livingstone and Ellen J. Helsper, 'Parental Mediation of Children's Internet Use', *Journal of Broadcasting and Electronic Media*, 52/4 (2008), p. 581.
24 Jessica L. Navarro and Michaeline Jensen, 'Styles of Digital Parental Mediation: A Multi-Group Person-Centered Approach', *Journal of Child and Family Studies*, 35/2 (February 2026), p. 485.
25 Navarro and Jensen, p. 481.
26 Raws, p. 39.
27 Livingstone and Helsper, 'Parental Mediation of Children's Internet Use', p. 581.
28 Celine Fox, Deirdre Robertson and Pete Lunn, *Parenting in a Digital Era: A Narrative Review*, ESRI Research Series 218 (Dublin, Economic and Social Research Institute, 2025), pp. 27–8.
29 Sonia Livingstone et al., 'Maximizing Opportunities and Minimizing Risks for Children Online: The Role of Digital Skills in Emerging Strategies of Parental Mediation', *Journal of Communication*, 67/1 (February 2017), p. 85.
30 Navarro and Jensen, p. 496.
31 Ellen Johanna Helsper, Giuseppe Alessandro Veltri and Sonia Livingstone, 'Parental Mediation of Children's Online Risks: The Role of Parental Risk

Perception, Digital Skills and Risk Experiences', *New Media and Society*, 27/11 (November 2025).

32 Livingstone et al., p. 85.

33 Livingstone and Blum-Ross, p. 33.

34 Matthias Bastian, 'Meta Can Use Public Facebook and Instagram Data for AI training, German Court Rules', The Decoder, 24 May 2025.

35 Jordan D. Alexander et al., 'Adolescent Smartphone Use, Sleep, and Physical Activity: Daily Associations between Sensor-based Measures in the Adolescent Brain Cognitive Development (ABCD) Study', *Psychiatry Research*, 349 (2025).

36 Fox, Robertson and Lunn, p. 24.

37 James Bridle, 'Something Is Wrong on the Internet', Medium, 6 November 2017.

38 Arijeta Lajka, 'How A.I.-Generated Videos are Distorting Your Child's YouTube Feed', *The New York Times*, 26 February 2026.

39 Mona Arthi Efcibha et al., 'Short Video Addiction and Its Impact on Cognitive Functioning in Adolescents and Youth: A Systematic Review', *International Journal of Adolescence and Youth*, 31/1 (2026).

40 Marianna Spring, 'How the "Red v Blue School Wars" Exposed the Social Media Gap between Children and Parents', BBC News, 10 March 2026.

41 HRH the Princess of Wales with Robert Waldinger, 'The Power of Human Connection in a Distracted World', Centre for Early Childhood, 9 October 2025.

42 Bernard Golden, '"Parental Phubbing" Is a Powerful Form of Disregard', Psychology Today (blog), 12 June 2025.

Conclusion

1 '*Artemis II* Astronaut Christina Koch: "Looking back at Earth ... it truly emphasized how alike we are"', *Popular Science*, 8 April 2026.

2 *Children's Media Lives 2025*, Ofcom/Revealing Reality, 2025, p. 4.

3 Kali Hays, Nardine Saad and Regan Morris, 'Campaigners welcome Meta and YouTube's defeat in landmark social media addiction trial', BBC News, 25 March 2026.

4 Zoe Kleninman, '"A Game-changing Moment for Social Media" – What Next for Big Tech After Landmark Addiction Verdict?', BBC News, 26 March 2026.

5 Steve Rose, '"Don't Pander to the Tech Giants!" How a Youth Movement for Digital Justice Is Spreading Across Europe', *Guardian*, 9 December 2025.